Teach Yourself VISUALLY™

Crafting
with Kids

Teach Yourself VISUALLY™

Crafting
with Kids

by Jennifer Casa

WILEY

Wiley Publishing, Inc.

Teach Yourself VISUALLY™ Crafting with Kids

For general information on our other products and services or to obtain technical support please contact our Customer Care Department within the U.S. at (877) 762-2974, outside the U.S. at (317) 572-3993 or fax (317) 572-4002.

Wiley also publishes its books in a variety of electronic formats. Some content that appears in print may not be available in electronic books. For more information about Wiley products, please visit our web site at www.wiley.com.

Library of Congress Control Number: 2011921208

ISBN: 978-0-470-64370-9

Printed in the United States of America

10   9   8   7   6   5   4   3   2   1

Book production by Wiley Publishing, Inc. Composition Services

Praise for the Teach Yourself VISUALLY Series

I just had to let you and your company know how great I think your books are. I just purchased my third Visual book (my first two are dog-eared now!) and, once again, your product has surpassed my expectations. The expertise, thought, and effort that go into each book are obvious, and I sincerely appreciate your efforts. Keep up the wonderful work!

—Tracey Moore (Memphis, TN)

I have several books from the Visual series and have always found them to be valuable resources.

—Stephen P. Miller (Ballston Spa, NY)

Thank you for the wonderful books you produce. It wasn't until I was an adult that I discovered how I learn—visually. Although a few publishers out there claim to present the material visually, nothing compares to Visual books. I love the simple layout. Everything is easy to follow. And I understand the material! You really know the way I think and learn. Thanks so much!

—Stacey Han (Avondale, AZ)

Like a lot of other people, I understand things best when I see them visually. Your books really make learning easy and life more fun.

—John T. Frey (Cadillac, MI)

I am an avid fan of your Visual books. If I need to learn anything, I just buy one of your books and learn the topic in no time. Wonders! I have even trained my friends to give me Visual books as gifts.

—Illona Bergstrom (Aventura, FL)

I write to extend my thanks and appreciation for your books. They are clear, easy to follow, and straight to the point. Keep up the good work! I bought several of your books and they are just right! No regrets! I will always buy your books because they are the best.

—Seward Kollie (Dakar, Senegal)

Credits

Acquisitions Editor
Pam Mourouzis

Senior Project Editor
Donna Wright

Copy Editor
Lynn Northrup

Editorial Manager
Christina Stambaugh

Vice President and Publisher
Cindy Kitchel

Vice President and Executive Publisher
Kathy Nebenhaus

Interior Design
Kathie Rickard
Elizabeth Brooks

Photography
Matt Bowen

Additional Photography
Jennifer Casa

Special Thanks...

To the following companies for supplying materials used in this book:

Clover Needlecraft, Inc.
www.clover-usa.com

Plaid Enterprises, Inc.
www.plaidonline.com

Ornamentea
www.ornamentea.com

About the Author

Jennifer Casa is a mama, homemaker, artist, designer, and maker of many things. She thinks a great day involves any combination of sewing, knitting, cooking, craft time with her kids, and rockin' out with her husband. She creates patterns and projects for crafters of all ages, and her work is featured regularly in online and print publications. She lives nestled between the city and the country in Ohio with her husband and twin daughters.

Visit JChandmade.typepad.com for more projects and inspiration.

Acknowledgments

I would like to thank my Agent, Linda Roghaar, for her tremendous support and encouragement, and for presenting me with this wonderful opportunity. I would also like to thank Pam Mourouzis and Cindy Kitchel for their guidance while writing this book. My sincere appreciation goes to Donna Wright for her professionalism, editorial expertise, and kindness throughout this project. Thanks also to Matt Bowen for excellent photography, as well as the entire team at Wiley for pulling this book together so marvelously.

Thanks to my friends and family—most especially my daughters—who prototyped each and every project, and cooperated with my requests for "just one more photo" over the course of the past year. I would also like to thank my parents for cheering on my creative endeavors ever since I was a child. A big thank you to all of my blog readers, who have shared kindness, inspiration and laughter for years. And thanks especially to Meg McElwee for a thoughtful late-night conversation that helped me navigate the road to becoming an author. Most of all, I want to thank my husband, Pat, for believing in me. You are surely special.

For Sophia and Natalie—you make my days sparkle. xoxo

Table of Contents

CHAPTER 3　Summer Vacation　40

CHAPTER 4　Back to School　72

Table of Contents

CHAPTER 5   Winter Wonderland   88

CHAPTER 6   Happy Holidays   104

Table of Contents

CHAPTER 1

Kid-Friendly Crafting in Your Home

Kids are amazing little teachers, and we are blessed to have them in our lives. The freedom with which they approach and delight in arts and crafts is truly inspiring. Children have the courage to innovate without fear of judgment or failure—a lesson from which we can all surely benefit. Celebrate creativity in your home by designating a kid-friendly craft space that everyone can share and enjoy.

Before you get started, there are a few things to consider—the amount of time you spend crafting, what materials are on hand, and how to best organize everything so it contributes to a positive atmosphere in your home rather creating clutter. This will make art and craft endeavors at home even more enjoyable experiences shared by you and your kids.

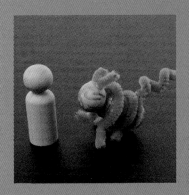 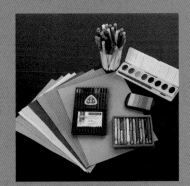 

Tune In to Your Kids

Crafting with children is about so much more than what you're making—it's about the conversations, the laughter, and the warmth you feel in your heart long after a project is complete. It's about the experience. Tune in to your kids' creative spirits, learn from them, and celebrate being in the moment.

LISTEN

Kids thrive when given the opportunity to do things by and for themselves, but they also need and desire guidance. An excellent way to provide that is to work side-by-side with them, encouraging their sense of discovery. You can support and nurture their independent spirits by simply listening—turn off your transmitter and turn on your receiver.

Kids can sometimes find it difficult to articulate and express themselves, making it even more important for us to be aware of nonverbal cues. Transitions can be especially challenging—the start of school, moving to a new city, the addition of a new baby, etc. Arts and crafts present a fantastic opportunity for you to share time together, soothe anxieties, express love, and be supportive. Let them do the talking and follow their lead—goodness knows, kids are incredibly creative, and they can teach us a great deal.

BE PLAYFUL

Just be. It sounds simple, right?

As adults, it is easy to become overwhelmed by our lengthy to-do lists. Even if things are not written down, we are somehow always aware of what needs to be done. This is yet another reason why it is so important to make time each day to be together without those distractions. If it will help you, write it on your to-do list— giving yourselves that shared creative time will enrich both you and your children.

Be reasonable. Choose projects you can accomplish within a given timeframe rather than try to rush something to completion. Your kids will learn the importance of delivering on one's promises. And just as much as they learn from us, we can learn from them.

Try something new. And never be afraid to make mistakes. Mistakes happen to all of us. Sometimes, really great things can happen when you take a detour. What happens *happens,* so ride the waves and see where they take you. Be in the moment.

ADAPT THE PROJECTS

This book is filled with projects that will appeal to kids of all ages. You can work on these projects as written, or simply use them as a springboard for your own creative endeavors. Encourage your kids to rethink, modify, and transform these projects into something of their own design.

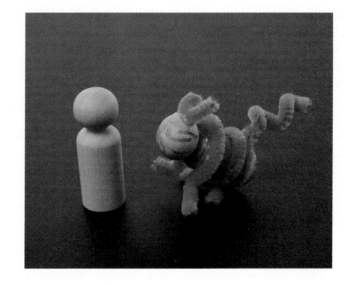

A great example of this is what happened while we were prototyping our family of peg pals (Chapter 9). My daughter noticed we had not included our cat among our family of peg pals—and without skipping a beat, she scampered off to the next room where I saw her turn a small peg on its side, and create our peg cat with a marker and a few pipe cleaners. She was so excited to share her surprise with us, and I was thrilled that she felt confident and empowered to make the project her own.

It is my sincere hope that you and your kids use this book as a springboard for your own creativity, and that you feel inspired to make the projects and activities your own.

Materials and Organization

There is no shortage of impressive craft supplies on the market. Your local arts and crafts store is a great resource, the aisles filled with a wide variety of quality craft materials. A simple starter project you can work on together is stocking your own craft bin, drawer, or entire cabinet at home. Consider your space, then discuss what interests your kids—perhaps there is a color, texture, shape, or crafting medium. Check around your home for materials you may already have on hand, and then stock up on basic supplies you will need.

ORGANIZATION AND STORAGE

In our home, we transformed what was our dining room sideboard into an awesome craft cabinet, and our dining room is now the main arts and crafts zone in our home. A bit untraditional, perhaps. But we considered our lifestyle and how we truly live in this space. We determined that heirloom dishes could be safely stored in the basement and brought up to be appreciated on special occasions when we use them. That said, you do not need to do this in your space—rather, I suggest that you assess your space as well as your lifestyle, and then create a solution that you can all enjoy and that will work for you. It does not matter if you have a single craft bin or an entire craft cabinet, as long as everything has a place.

STORAGE SOLUTIONS

Clear storage bins with lids are great because they allow you to see what is inside each container before opening it. But you do not need to spend a dime on storage bins if you prefer not to. Reuse cardboard shoe boxes, canisters, and so on, paint or cover them with decorative paper, and clearly label the contents. Store like items together. Place tapes, glues, and fasteners in one bin, fill another with felt scraps, and yet another can hold craft foam stickers. Save clear plastic to-go containers—after a thorough washing, they work great for storing art supplies.

ORGANIZE YOUR CRAFT SPACE

Get down to your kids' level—I mean that quite literally. Think about how they will interact with the materials and space, and put your arts and crafts storage area at their height. Use storage containers that they can easily maneuver independently. And remember to keep all your materials and tools age-appropriate.

BASICS

A great start is to have a variety of papers, and an assortment of good-quality crayons, colored pencils, or markers. Stamp pads are fun for everyone, whether used with store-bought stamps or originals you have carved from erasers. A small watercolor set travels well and encourages creative expression while on-the-go. (See the first photo).

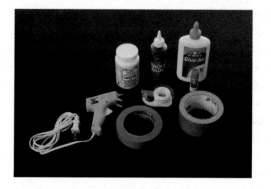

There are many adhesives available, all with different applications. White glue is terrific for paper crafts; thicker craft glue is better when working with felt, fabric, or foam; hot glue dries quickly and offers a secure bond; and glue sticks are simple to use at any age. Scotch tape and painters' tape are also nice to have on hand, and duct tape is incredibly versatile.

To protect your work surface, use a piece of oilcloth, a vinyl tablecloth, or simply lay out some newspapers. A bucket is great for mixing, blending, dyeing, and even washing up after working with outdoor crafts.

ESSENTIAL TOOLS FROM AROUND THE HOUSE

Cutting develops fine motor skills and hand-eye coordination, so be sure to have good scissors in age-appropriate sizes. Rulers are excellent measuring tools and also help young hands draw straight lines. A single-hole punch can be used not only with paper, but also on plastic and lightweight fabrics.

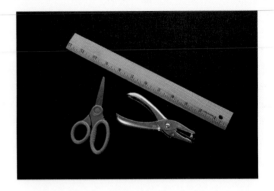

Have a few different kinds of paintbrushes, including fine, medium, and broad tip, as well as foam applicators. You can easily wash these and use them over and over. Paint stir sticks are handy for stirring, scooping, digging, and building, and also provide a nice straight edge. Needle nose pliers are useful in twisting wire, as well as picking up small items in tight spots. And keep your stapler filled with staples.

Measuring spoons and cups are valuable tools not only for cooking, but for arts and crafts as well. A wooden spoon, butter knife, and chopsticks are terrific for stirring, mixing, pressing, smoothing, and even cutting soft clay. Consider setting aside a few kitchen utensils specifically for arts and crafts.

TOOLS FOR YOUR WISH LIST

A good set of alphabet stamps can be used to apply ink to paper or fabric, as well as make impressions in clay. A screw punch is similar to a single-hole punch; however, it can create a hole from any angle and is not limited by the edge of a paper. A craft knife or rotary cutter and self-healing mat can be very precise, but both are incredibly sharp and best used by adults.

A few other fun items you might want to consider investing in include a good-quality weaving loom, pompom makers, craft punches, and a needle-felting tool and mat.

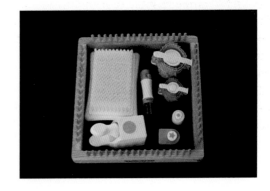

SUPPLIES FROM THE RECYCLING BIN

Think outside the box—chances are your home is already well-stocked with free craft materials.

Something as simple as cardboard tubes from paper towels and toilet paper rolls can be transformed into telescopes, marble runs, snorkels, antennae, tunnels for tiny play figures, or sliding boards on a playground made of building blocks. Newspaper is also a handy material to keep around—not only is it great for protecting your work surface from drips and spills, but it can also be painted and transformed into something new. Milk cartons can be washed, disassembled, and repurposed. Small bottles and jars make great storage for leftover paint and glue. And small, clean plastic containers from yogurt or pudding are useful for blending paint, rinsing brushes, and organizing small tools or supplies.

Accessibility and Cleanup

An important part of creating a kid-friendly craft space is taking necessary safety precautions. Consider the ages of the kids who will use these materials, as well as those who may interact with them, even if only in passing. Taking preventive measures when establishing your craft space will create a more comfortable and functional environment for everyone.

MAKE IT ACCESSIBLE

Depending on the configuration of your craft area, you will want to determine what you would like your kids to be able to access independently. Be reasonable with your choices and try not to overwhelm kids with too many craft materials at once. Rotate materials on a regular basis to stimulate their interests. You may even want to take some time after your kids are in bed to set up a certain craft for the next day. Bookmark a project and assemble all the necessary materials, and when they rise and shine the following morning, follow their lead.

MAKE IT SAFE

Be sure to store larger and possibly harmful materials out of reach of children. Items like a hot glue gun, wire snips, pliers, and a craft knife are best stored in a separate area that only adults can access, and pulled out for use on craft projects together. If you have small children, you will also want to store items such as paint, plaster, and adhesives separately.

MESSES HAPPEN

It's true. Paint will spill, markers will bleed through onto things, and glue will end up where you would rather it not. But messes don't have to be a big deal. Teach your kids how to clean up after themselves by examples. We keep a low drawer stocked with clean dishrags and towels so they are at the ready when the need for cleanup arises.

Just relax and have fun.

Enjoy the process.

And enjoy each other.

Happy crafting!

CHAPTER 2

Spring Cleaning

Springtime brings with it an urge to clean out and spruce up our home. In this chapter, we use readily available materials—and a few surprising ones, at that—to start fresh and celebrate the season. These simple and fun home décor projects are sure to liven up and brighten your home. Enjoy!

What's Your Fabric Sign?

Personalize any space in your home with original fabric-wrapped wire signs. They are simple to make, and your kids will especially enjoy adding their own special tags to their rooms. Whip up one special sign, or an entire alphabet to create an interchangeable piece. They will bring a new energy to your surroundings, whether you use them for specific celebrations or year-round décor.

Let's Make It

Time: Approx. 15 minutes per letter

MATERIALS

- Scrap paper and a pencil
- Aluminum jewelry wire (12-gauge)
- Wire snips (used for jewelry making)
- Needle nose pliers
- Fabric in a variety of prints and colors
- Quilt batting scraps (or an old sweatshirt)
- Scissors
- Low-temp hot glue gun (or craft glue)

CREATE THE WRAPPED LETTERS

1. Sketch how you would like your letters to appear on pieces of scrap paper. Play with the size, shape, and scale of the letters until you are happy with your template.

2. Use your sketch to estimate how much wire you need for the first letter and cut it.

3. Shape the wire into letter form with your hands. If necessary, cut additional pieces of wire to complete each letter shape.

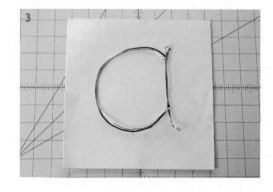

4. Cut the fabrics and quilt batting scraps (or an old sweatshirt) into 1"-wide strips.

5. Place a small amount of glue on the end of one of the batting strips and begin winding it around the wire letter, overlapping your wraps slightly as you go. When you reach the end of the strip, add another drop of glue to secure it to itself and the form.

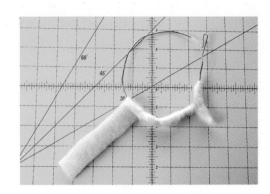

6. Continue to work in this manner as you wrap the entire form with batting to create a sturdy letter that is still pliable.

7. Repeat this process using the fabric strips until the letter is wrapped in fabric.

8. Shape the letter with your hands until you are pleased with the final look.

9. Repeat this entire process with the remaining letters on your sketch.

TIP

Display Options

There are many ways you can display your signs.

- Suspend each letter from the ceiling using fishing wire to create a floating sign.

- Scatter the individual letters of your sign above a doorway and secure them in place with small tack nails.

- Paint a ¼" dowel so it will blend in with the wall color. Secure each letter of the sign to the dowel rod with a small dot of glue and tie with invisible thread. Rest both ends of the dowel on two small tack nails in the wall.

Eggciting Flower Wreath

Add a seasonal splash of color to your front door with this cheery floral wreath. In just a few simple steps, you and your kids will transform materials from the recycling bin into an array of springtime flowers that is sure to brighten everyone's day.

Let's Make It

Measurement: 12" in circumference ● **Time:** 1 hour

MATERIALS

- 12"-square of sturdy cardboard (a clean pizza box lid works great)
- Pencil
- 12" dinner plate and a smaller salad plate (approximately 8")
- Scissors

- Acrylic paints and paintbrushes
- Fabric scraps
- Egg carton (for 1 dozen eggs) made of cardboard-type material
- Low-temp hot glue gun (or craft glue)
- Embroidery floss, yarn, fishing wire, or twine

MAKE THE WREATH FORM

1. Trace a 12" circle onto the cardboard with a pencil using the dinner plate as a guide.

2. Use the salad plate to trace a smaller circle centered inside the larger one.

3. Cut out the wreath form.

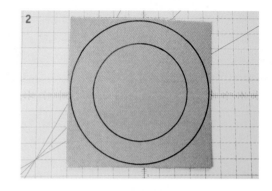

4. Paint both sides of the wreath form using acrylic paint. Try a color similar to where it will be displayed—the finished wreath will appear to float on the surface.

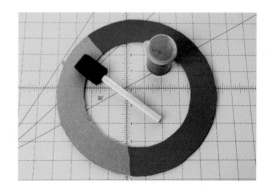

CREATE THE FLOWERS

5. Cut out a dozen 4"–5" circles from fabric scraps. Measurements do not need to be precise; rough, wavy edges can be pretty—have fun with it.

6. Cut out the small "cups" from the bottom of the egg carton. Trim off any jagged edges.

7. Paint each of these cups with acrylic paints in colors that coordinate with your fabrics. Allow to dry.

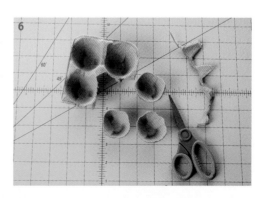

ASSEMBLE THE FLOWERS

8 Dot some glue on the bottom of one of the painted egg cups.

9 Center one of the smaller fabric circles on the bottom of the egg cup with the right side of the fabric facing up.

10 Place a few dots of glue around the outside top edge of the egg cup and bring the fabric up to create the look of ruffled flower petals.

11 Continue working in this manner until you have created a dozen flowers.

12 If you like, you can create fuller flowers by layering a second, slightly larger circle of fabric on each blossom.

ASSEMBLE THE WREATH

13 Place the flowers on the wreath form and arrange them in a layout you like.

14 Glue each of the flowers to the wreath form and hang it up with a length of embroidery floss or yarn.

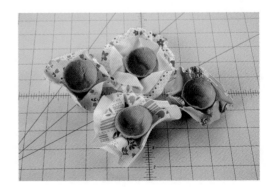

Make this cool and incredibly useful interactive calendar for your home using wool felt and a few fun craft tools. As the kids switch out the date each morning, they can actively organize their day with special activity pieces customized for them.

Let's Make It

Measurement: 9" x 18" ● **Time:** 1–2 hours

MATERIALS

- 3mm wool felt (9" x 18" sheet)
- ³/₈" grommets and grommet pliers
- Two 1" buttons
- Needle and thread
- Craft knife or scissors

- Wool felt (craft weight) or flannel in a variety of colors
- Alphabet rubber stamps (¹/₄"–¹/₂" in size)
- Multicolored pigment ink pad
- Glue
- Ruler and pencil

MAKE THE MAIN DOCKET

1 With the 3mm felt piece in portrait position, place a
³/₈" grommet in both of the top corners following the
manufacturer's instructions in the grommet kit.

2 Stitch two 1" buttons onto the felt 7" up from the
bottom and 1" in from either side.

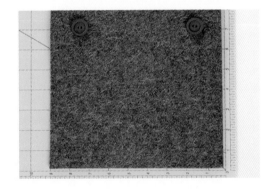

3 Use a craft knife (or scissors) to slice two "buttonholes" in the felt. They should each be 1" long, and
positioned 1" from the bottom edge and 1" in from
either side.

4 Fold the bottom of the 3mm felt upward and fasten the buttons through the buttonholes. This creates a rounded pocket to store the docket pieces that are not in use on any given day.

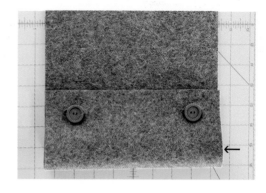

CREATE THE CALENDAR

5 Cut 1"-wide strips of the craft-weight felt or flannel.

6 Use the alphabet stamps to print each of the days of the week and the months onto the felt strips.

7 Trim each of the days and months to size.

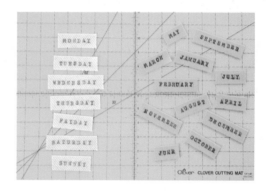

8 Cut out 1" numbers from the craft-weight felt or flannel to use for the date each day. You will need #0–9, and then also another of #1–2.

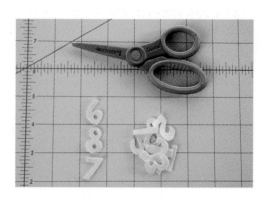

9. Cut out the letters "TODAY IS."

10. Glue "TODAY IS" to the top of the docket, using a ruler for even placement.

CUSTOMIZE YOUR ACTIVITY PIECES

11. Use the alphabet stamps to personalize a few of the strips with activities that your kids participate in regularly.

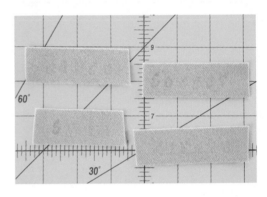

FYI

Put Your Daily Docket to Work

This piece is very lightweight, so you can hang your daily docket on two small nails or push-pins in the wall. Use a level to make sure it is straight before hammering in the nails.

As the kids update the calendar each morning, they can also switch their activity pieces to review and organize the day ahead. All of the unused pieces can be stored in the bottom folded pocket.

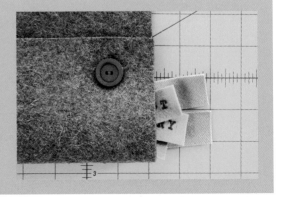

Storing your kids' art in these personalized boxes is a great way to organize as well as document their growth and maturity. Because the boxes are flat, they can easily be stored under beds during the current school year, and then later stacked in the basement or attic. Sort through them with your kids and downsize their collection every few years, but be sure to save the cover art.

Let's Make It

Measurement: 26½" x 19" x 3" ● **Time:** 1 hour

MATERIALS

- One sheet pizza box per child (available from your local pizzeria)
- Permanent marker
- Watercolor paints and paintbrushes

TRACE YOUR CHILD

1. Place the unfolded pizza box flat on the floor with the outer side facing up.

2. Have your kids lay on top of their pizza boxes with their heads positioned on the top side of the box.

3. Trace around your kids with a permanent marker.

4. Have your kids write their names and ages on their box tops using permanent marker.

5. Set out watercolor paints, paintbrushes, and plenty of water for your kids so they can paint their self-portraits on their boxes.

6. Allow to dry completely before folding into box form and using for art storage.

Suncatcher Strands

These colorful "beaded" dangles add a splash of color to a sunny window. They are simple to make and can be easily adapted to suit any room, season, or occasion. Whether you make them for a birthday party or "just because," these suncatchers are bound to make everyone smile.

Let's Make It

Time: ½ hour

MATERIALS
- Tissue paper in a variety of colors
- Scissors
- Clear self-adhesive laminate contact paper
- Needle and thread (or sewing machine)

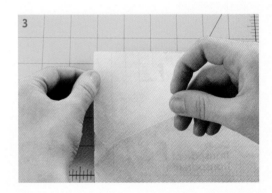

CREATE THE SUNCATCHERS

1. Cut small squares of tissue paper.

2. Cut a piece of contact paper about the size of a place mat.

3. Peel off the paper backing and place the sheet with the adhesive side up.

4. Place small pieces of the colored tissue paper onto the contact paper. They will stick to the adhesive right away.

5. Continue in this manner, covering the entire sheet with tissue papers and overlapping them in a color combination you like.

6 Cut another piece of contact paper the same size as the first.

7 Peel off the paper backing and stick the clear contact paper on top of the one covered with tissue papers. You will be placing them sticky side to sticky side, sandwiching the tissue papers in between.

8 Smooth your hands over the suncatcher sheet to work out any bubbles.

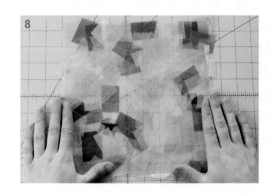

9 Cut out a variety of shapes from the suncatcher material. Simple circles and squares work great, but you can get as fancy as you like—raindrops, leaves, wavy lines—look out the window for inspiration. Try using decorative craft punches, if you like.

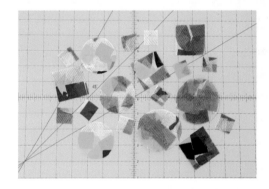

10 Once you have assembled a pile of suncatcher shapes, stitch them together using a needle and thread or your sewing machine. Leave a few inches of thread between each of the suncatchers.

11 Dangle the suncatcher strands over curtain rods, string them as a party garland, or simply tape them to a window frame.

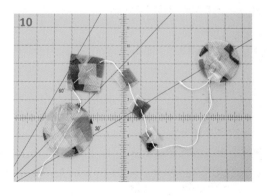

Patchwork Lanterns

Celebrate your favorite prints and patterns by making these floating patchwork lanterns. Dangle a few in a bedroom, string them under a picnic umbrella, drape a strand across a doorway, or use them to decorate for a party. This project would be a fun activity for kids to create their own party favors to take home and enjoy long after the party is over.

Let's Make It

Time: ½ hour plus drying time overnight

MATERIALS

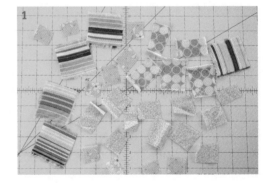

- Fabric scraps
- Scissors
- Balloons
- Empty canisters (such as for coffee or oatmeal)
- Old tablecloth or wax paper
- Empty yogurt containers
- Mod Podge or white glue
- Foam brushes

PREPARE YOUR MATERIALS

1. Cut the fabrics into various small shapes.

2. Blow up a balloon and tie a knot in the end.

3. Rest the balloon in an empty canister to create a steady work surface.

4. Spread out an old tablecloth or some wax paper to protect your work surface.

5. Fill a small yogurt container with a ¼ cup of Mod Podge or white glue and dilute it with a spoonful of water. Stir gently to mix.

MAKE THE LANTERNS

6 Use a foam brush to apply a thin layer of the adhesive directly to the balloon's surface.

7 One at a time, place a fabric scrap onto the balloon. Smooth out any air bubbles with your fingers.

8 Spread another thin layer of the adhesive directly on top of the fabric.

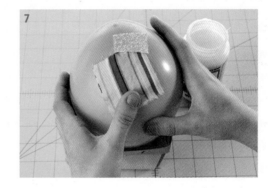

9 Continue in this fashion to cover the entire balloon with a patchwork of fabric pieces. Shift the balloon's position on the canister as needed to work on other areas, as well as to make sure it is not sticking to the canister.

10 Hang it to dry overnight. Knot a string around the balloon tie and suspend it from a shower curtain rod or the wash line outside.

CROSS YOUR FINGERS AND SEE IF IT WORKED

11 You want the fabric to be completely dry and stiff to the touch. If it is not completely dry, it will collapse. My kids and I know this from experience—and it was sad. Be patient and wait until the patchwork is completely dry.

12 Pierce the balloon with something sharp. Do not be surprised if it doesn't make a significant "popping" sound. The balloon often tends to slowly collapse within the patchwork lantern and peels away from the fabric on its own. Again, be patient.

13

13 Don't worry if the patchwork squishes in a little bit, Insert a new balloon into the patchwork and inflate it. When the lantern is round again, just let the air out of the new balloon and remove it.

Hang Up the Lanterns

- Tie a few lanterns with string, embroidery floss, or fishing wire to suspend them from a cup hook in the ceiling.

- Space out several smaller lanterns along a length of bias binding or ribbon to create a festive garland to hang for a party.

- Dangle a bunch of individual patchwork lanterns from your picnic table umbrella with varying lengths of fishing wire.

Great Impression Family Tree

Create this sweet family heirloom to keep or give as a gift to someone you love. Kids will love seeing their fingerprints bring this family tree to life in this simple and quick project.

Let's Make It

Time: ½–1 hour

MATERIALS

- Watercolor paper (ours measures 11" x 15")
- Watercolor paints and brush
- Multicolored ink pad
- Fine-point permanent marker

CREATE THE FAMILY TREE

1. Work together with your kids to create a rough sketch of your family tree. You can make it as simple or as elaborate as you like. Discuss how many people will be on the family tree and how they are related.

2. Use the watercolors to paint your personal family tree shape onto the watercolor paper. Allow the paint to dry.

3. Press a finger into the ink pad and then onto the paper to indicate family members.

4. Repeat step 3 for everyone who is to be represented on the family tree. Group families together accordingly on different branches of the tree. Allow the ink to dry.

5. Use a fine-point permanent marker to write the names or initials of each person on the family tree.

Mod Mobiles

These mobiles are cool and modern enough to appeal to kids of all ages. Play with the felt to create your own signature pieces to display alone or in a grouping.

Let's Make It

Measurement: 18" ● **Time:** ½ hour

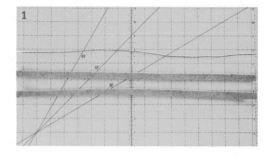

MATERIALS

- 3mm wool felt (9" x 18" sheets)
- Rotary cutter or scissors
- Ruler and pencil
- Aluminum jewelry wire (12-gauge)
- Wire snips (used for jewelry making)
- Needle nose pliers
- Low-temp hot glue gun (or craft glue)

DO ALL YOUR CUTTING FIRST

1. Cut ½" strips of the felt measuring 18" long.

2. Cut an 18" length of the wire with the snips.

MAKE THE WIRED STRAND

3. Take one felt strip and run glue down the center of the entire piece.

4. Place the wire in the glue and let it dry.

5. Apply some more glue on top of the wire and then place a second strip of felt on top. This looks like a long skinny sandwich of felt with a wire secretly nestled inside.

MAKE YOUR MOD CONCENTRIC CIRCLES

6 Use a pencil to make a mark at 4" and another mark at 10" on a felt strip.

7 Form a 4" circle with the strip and glue it in place. (If you notice it is taking awhile to dry, use a clothespin to hold it in place for a few minutes.)

8 Form a 6" circle around the 4" circle (using the mark at 10" as a guide) and glue it in place.

9 Form the final 8" circle around the 6" circle and glue it in place.

10 Repeat this process to create several more mod circles. Make them in the same color, or whip up a bunch in a variety of colors.

7

FINISHING

11 Glue your mod circles to the wired strip at regular intervals.

12 Twist the ends of the wired felt strip to create a "hook" for hanging.

13 Twist the entire mobile to create movement and visual interest.

14 Hang it up in your room, or make a bunch to create a larger mobile installation.

9

11

Have fun with it—try different-sized strips of felt, and try forming different shapes with the wired felt strand.

31

Window and Wall Decals

Repositionable decals are simple to make and a great way for kids to personalize their space. Use this simple process to create one-of-a-kind decals that won't damage your windows or walls. Try this project as a fun party activity so kids can create something special to take home.

Let's Make It

Time: ½ hour

MATERIALS

- Clear self-adhesive laminate contact paper (be sure it is "repositionable" and not permanent adhesive)
- Painter's tape (or masking tape)
- Acrylic paints and paintbrushes
- Scissors
- Image templates (use stencils, books, magazines, or draw your own)
- Permanent marker

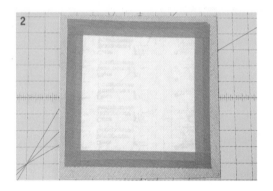

CREATE THE DECAL

1. Cut a piece of the contact paper larger than the size of the decal you wish to make.

2. Place the contact paper with the paper side down and tape it to your work surface around the edges.

3. Choose two complementary colors of paint and place a small amount of each on a palette (or plate) for your child to work with.

4. Paint the entire surface of the contact paper using a variety of brush strokes.

5. Allow the paint to dry, then remove the tape.

6. Cut another piece of contact paper the same size as the first.

7. Peel the paper backing off the unpainted piece of contact paper and carefully stick it right on top of the painted piece.

8. Smooth out any air bubbles with your hands.

9. Use a permanent marker to trace your image template on the decal material.

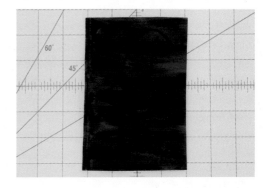

10. Cut out the decal.

11. Remove the paper backing from each decal and stick your creations to a window or onto the wall.

Letter Tiles

Combine a series of these fun letter tiles to create whimsical customized signs that will look fantastic over their beds, in a playroom or book nook, or to designate an area within a room.

Let's Make It

Time: 1–2 hours plus drying time

MATERIALS

- Empty shoeboxes and their lids (you will need one shoebox or lid per letter)
- Fabric in a variety of prints and patterns
- Old tablecloth
- Scissors
- Mod Podge
- Foam brushes
- Pencil
- Acrylic paints and paintbrushes

MAKE A PLAN

1. Lay out the boxes and lids on the floor with the open side down to determine the placement of each letter in the finished piece. Alternate lids and boxes so that some of the letters will pop, position some horizontally and others vertically, place small ones in between larger ones, and so on.

2. When you are happy with the placement of the boxes, pick them up one at a time and write the corresponding letter inside of the box for reference. It is also helpful to draw directional arrows or write "this end up" inside each box one for reference when painting.

3. Determine which fabric you will use to cover each box or lid. Place the fabrics inside of each box until you are ready to cover it.

COVER THE BOXES

4 Set an old tablecloth on your work surface.

5 Lay out your fabric for the first box face down and then place the bottom of the box on the fabric.

6 Cut the fabric to size so that it will extend to cover the sides of the box or lid.

7 Turn the box over and spread a thick even layer of the Mod Podge over the entire flat surface of the bottom with a foam brush.

8 Place the fabric right side up on top of the sticky surface and smooth out any air bubbles with your hands.

9 Apply another coat of Mod Podge on top of the fabric with the foam brush.

10 Allow to dry completely.

⑪ Cut out a small square from each corner of the fabric. This will help to create smooth, even corners and allow the fabric to lie flat.

⑫ Working one side at a time, spread some Mod Podge on a box side. Then apply the fabric in the same manner you did for the main side.

⑬ Apply some Mod Podge to the fabric at each corner with a foam brush and smooth out the seams with your fingers. The fabric should overlap slightly onto the other side.

⑭ Allow to dry completely.

⑮ Trim the fabric so that it is flush with the open rim of the box.

⑯ Repeat this process with each of the boxes/lids and their corresponding fabrics. You will end up with fabric-covered wall tiles.

PAINT THE LETTERS ONTO THE TILES

⑰ Use a pencil to outline each of the letters onto the boxes and lids. You can draw these freehand, or print stencils on the computer if you prefer.

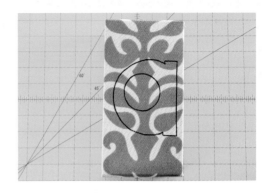

⑱ Use a paintbrush to carefully paint in each letter using acrylic paints. You can apply different colors to each tile, or use one color that coordinates with all the fabrics.

⑲ Allow to dry completely.

TIP

Hanging the Letter Tiles

These letter tiles are really lightweight and super easy to display. Work one tile at a time and step back now and then to check the placement of each. Pencil a tiny mark on the wall before hammering in a small nail. Set the tiles on the nails and use a level to make sure each is even.

Smile! You're on the Chore Chart

$\int$ nap candid pictures of the kids doing their chores to create a fun twist on the traditional family chore chart. Helping around the house has never been so much fun!

Let's Make It

Measurement: about 15" x 20" ● **Time:** 1–2 hours

MATERIALS

- Camera (preferably a digital camera for which you have photo paper and a printer ready to go)
- Self-adhesive blank file folder labels
- Markers, crayons, or colored pencils
- 1 piece of fabric measuring about 15" x 20" for the chart (or as large as you like)
- Fabric or felt scraps
- Scissors
- Blank envelopes (1 per child)
- Laminator (we go to the local copy shop)
- Self-adhesive hook and loop dots

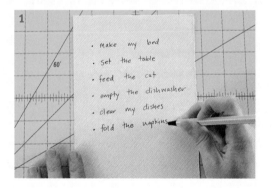

MAKE THE CHART ITEMS

1. Work with your kids to write a list of their responsibilities for helping around the house.

2. Take a picture of your kids doing each of the chores on their lists.

3. Print all of the photos.

④ Cut off the flap from each of the envelopes. (This is where they will store their chore cards when they are completed.)

⑤ Laminate the photos, fabric, and envelopes.

⑥ Use a scissors to carefully break the seal of the laminating on the envelope opening.

⑦ Have the kids write each of their chores on a blank file folder label.

⑧ Stick each label onto the bottom of their corresponding photographs.

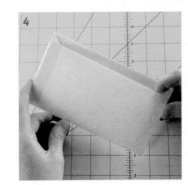

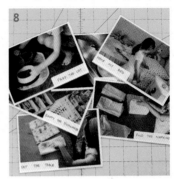

ASSEMBLE THE CHART

⑨ Cut out the kids' initials from scrap pieces of contrasting fabric or felt.

⑩ Create a column for each person by gluing their initials across the top of the chart.

⑪ Use hook and loop dots to attach each envelope to the chart at the bottom of his or her column.

⑫ Apply a scratchy-sided hook and loop dot to the back of each photo.

⑬ Apply a series of soft-sided hook and loop dots to the chart. Be sure that you are using one side of the hook and look dots for the photos, and the other side for the chart.

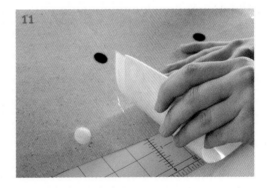

⑭ Kids can take their daily and weekly chores out of the envelopes and post them on the chart using the hook and loop dots.

⑮ As tasks are completed, they can remove them and place them into their envelopes for storage until the next time.

CHAPTER 3

Summer Vacation

Summer is all about fun in the sun, being outside, and enjoying nature in its full glory. We kick off this chapter with a countdown calendar you can put together as soon as the kids start talking about summertime. All of the projects in this chapter are intended to be enjoyed outdoors in between swinging, running through the sprinkler, and sipping something cool while admiring your creations. Have fun!

Summer Fun Countdown Calendar

The end of the school year is always exciting—kids are filled with anticipation of fun summer adventures in their near future. Let's tap in to that enthusiasm in this project, which functions like an advent calendar and incorporates your family's own list of favorite summertime activities. Think of it as a decorative summer "to do" list.

Let's Make It

Time: 1 hour

MATERIALS

- Scratch paper and pencils
- Double-sided decorative papers (such as scrapbooking paper)
- Scissors
- Markers of different colors
- 2 yards of medium rick rack
- 2 colors of embroidery floss, string, or twine
- Single-hole punch

MAKE A SUMMER FUN LIST

1. About a month or so before school is out, brainstorm with your kids to create a list of activities they would like to do this summer.

2. Cut out a variety of circles from the decorative papers. You need as many circles as there are items on your list.

3. Use different-colored markers to write each item from your summer fun list on a circle.

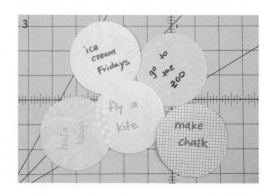

CREATE THE COUNTDOWN GARLAND

④ Lay out the rick rack in a straight line.

⑤ Take one color of embroidery floss and cut lengths varying from 5"–8". You need one strand for each item of the list.

⑥ Punch a hole through the top center and bottom center of each circle.

⑦ Slip a strand of floss through the top hole of one of the circles and make a knot.

⑧ Tie the circle to the rick rack, letting it dangle a bit.

⑨ Repeat step 8 with all of the circles, spacing them evenly across the length of rick rack. What you have at this point looks like a garland of your summer fun list.

⑩ Using the second color of embroidery floss, cut one 12" length for each circle.

⑪ Take a circle and bend the bottom upward with the writing toward the inside. Do not crease or fold the circle, just let it bend and align the hole from the bottom with the one at the top.

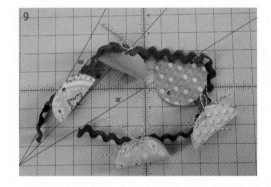

⑫ Slip a strand of the contrasting floss through both holes and tie a bow. The writing should be obscured from view, and what you have now is a garland of little dangling treasures.

⑬ Write numbers on each circle, if you like.

⑭ Each day during the month before school is out, untie one of the bows from a circle to reveal something fun to come in summertime.

TIP

Keep Track of What You Do!

Throughout the summer, as you do all of these fun things, untie them from the garland and post them with photos on the family bulletin board, in a scrapbook, or in a photo album.

Beach Towel Duffel Bag

C reate this great big duffel bag to carry all of your gear to and from the beach. In a few simple steps, you can transform a flat beach towel into a carry-all that is meant to get wet and sandy. At the end of the day, simply shake it out and hang it to dry on the line until tomorrow.

Let's Make It

Measurement: 30" x 30" ● **Time:** 1 hour

MATERIALS

- Beach towel (ours is 30" x 60", but any size cotton beach towel will work fine)
- Needle and thread (or a sewing machine)
- Ruler
- ³⁄₈" grommets and grommet pliers
- Straight pins
- 2 yards of cotton cording or thin rope

MAKE THE BEACH BAG

1. Wash and dry the towel thoroughly.

2. Fold the towel in half short end to short end, with the right sides together. The folded piece measures 30" x 30".

3. Stitch both sides of the towel together with a needle and thread (or sewing machine), using about a ¹⁄₂" seam allowance. Backstitch at the beginning and end of the line of stitches.

4. Turn the bag right side out.

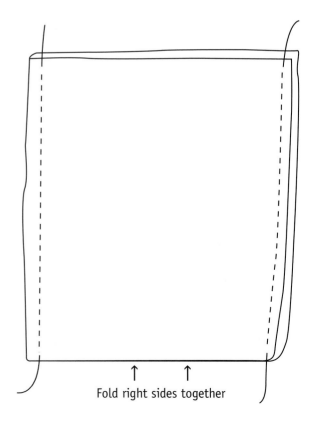

Fold right sides together

5. Place the bag flat on your work surface so you are looking at one of the side seams.

6. Follow the manufacturer's instructions in the grommet kit to place a ³/₈" grommet on either side of the seam that is 2" in from the seam and 2" down from the top edge.

7. Turn the bag inside out.

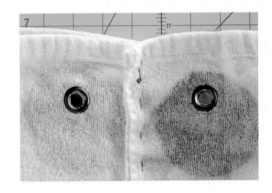

8. Roll down the top edge of the bag 1½" and pin in place. This seam will create a casing for the drawstring.

9. Stitch the drawstring casing in place (on the wrong side) using the edge of the towel as a guide for stitching.

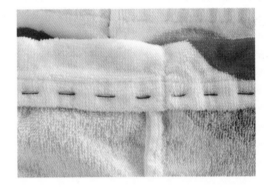

10. Turn the bag right side out.

11. Feed the cotton cording into one grommet and through the entire casing around the top of the bag. Pull the cording out through the other grommet and knot both ends together.

12. Toss your sand buckets, shovels, and all your sandcastle gear into the bag, pull the cord, and hit the beach.

Dip-Dyed T-Shirts

A great way to introduce kids to the magical process of dyeing fabric is by transforming plain white t-shirts into colorful, one-of-a-kind wearable art. In this project we start by dip-dyeing using kid-friendly fabric dyes. Once you learn a few simple steps, you will all be hooked on dyeing.

Let's Make It

Time: 2–3 hours plus laundering time

MATERIALS

- White t-shirts (100% cotton or 50% cotton/50% polyester)
- Permanent fabric dye (We are using Dylon permanent fabric dye, a commercial dye that reacts with warm (not boiling) water and salt. It is kid-friendly and readily available in a broad spectrum of colors.)
- Stainless steel sink, pot, or a large bucket
- Stainless steel tongs (optional)
- Rubber gloves

PREPARE THE MATERIALS

1. Weigh your fabric. If you do not have a kitchen scale, a safe estimate is that two children's t-shirts (or one adult t-shirt) weigh about 8 oz./½ lb. The dye we are using calls for one package per each ½ lb. of fabric.

2. Wash the t-shirts and leave them damp.

3. Put on your rubber gloves and prepare the dye bath according to the manufacturer's instructions on the dye package.

DIP-DYE YOUR SHIRTS

4 Determine how you would like your two main colors to appear on your finished shirt and how much you would like them to blend. Drawing a sketch ahead of time can help you all visualize finished shirts.

5 Rest your shirt on the edge of the sink/dye pot so that it is partially submerged.

5

6 Gently move the part of the t-shirt that is in the dye pot with your rubber-glove–covered hand or stainless steel tongs. Be careful not to drip any dye onto the rest of the shirt—or on yourself, the floor, or anywhere else, for that matter.

7 The dye we use says to stir the fabric in the dye for 15 minutes, then occasionally over the course of an hour. We took a more leisurely approach and stirred it very gently about every 10 minutes over the course of an hour.

8 After an hour (or the time recommended by the dye manufacturer), remove your shirt from the dye bath and gently squeeze out any excess dye. Again, wear your rubber gloves and be careful not to drip any of the dye onto the rest of the shirt.

9

9 Rinse the shirt according to the manufacturer's instructions. To make sure that all of the dye is out of the shirt, hand-wash your shirt in the sink (shown in bucket here) using a gentle detergent (we used baby shampoo).

10 Repeat this entire process with the second color of dye on the rest of the shirt. This step will dye the other section of the shirt and blend the two colors slightly where they meet.

11 You can also over-dye the entire shirt to create a blended overdyed shirt.

12 You can also mix dyes to create custom colors. Be sure to check the manufacturer's instructions and restrictions regarding color mixing. Consult a color wheel to review basic color principles—the possibilities are endless.

TRY THESE SIMPLE TIE-DYEING METHODS

⑬ Once you are comfortable with the basic process of using these dyes, you can create fun tie-dyed shirts by wrapping rubber bands tightly around different sections of your damp t-shirt before immersing it in the dye. Remove the rubber bands during hand-washing and machine wash as you did for the dip-dyed shirts.

⑭ Tie random knots over the entire shirt with rubber bands and dye once to create circles.

⑮ To create white stripes on a dyed shirt, lay the shirt out, and then roll it up either bottom-up, top-down, or side-to-side. Tie rubber bands every few inches the entire length of the rolled shirt.

⑯ Remove a few of the rubber bands after the first rinse, then over-dye the shirt to create multicolored circles or stripes.

Sun-Printed Go Fish Game

Sun prints are simple to make using everyday art materials. With a little planning and a lot of sunshine, you can put together a collection of cards to play with all year long. (Go Fish is a great game to sharpen listening and concentration skills for kids of all ages.)

Let's Make It

Measurement: 3" x 4" ● **Time:** 1 day of bright sunshine

MATERIALS

- Construction paper in dark colors
- 10 small stencils
- 20 blank 4" x 6" index cards
- Scissors
- Glue
- Permanent marker

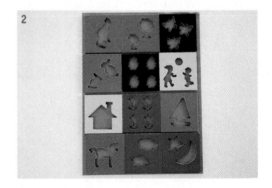

MAKE THE SUN PRINTS

1. Lay out a few sheets of dark construction paper in a bright and sunny spot.

2. Place the different stencils on top of the papers.

3. Leave to fade in the sun for at least an hour.

4. Remove the stencils from the papers. Areas that were exposed to the sun will have faded while those that were covered by the stencil will remain saturated with color.

5. Repeat this process three more times to create a total of 40 small sun prints (4 each from 10 different stencils).

CREATE THE CARD SET

6 Cut the index cards in half to create 40 cards that measure 3" x 4" each.

7 Cut out each of the sun prints and glue one onto each card.

8 Write on each card what the sun print is.

9 When finished, you will have created 40 cards—4 each of 10 different sun prints.

You are ready to play Go Fish!

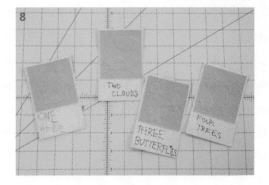

Let's Play

- The goal of the game is to collect as many sets of four sun prints as possible.

- Shuffle the cards.

- Deal five cards face down to each player.

- Spread the rest of the cards face down on your play area. This is the fish pond.

- Everyone picks up their cards and holds them so that no one else can see them.

- Starting with the player to the dealer's left, that person chooses one other person and asks him if he has a certain card. (For example, "Do you have one house?")

- If the player has any of those cards, he gives them to the person who asked. If not, he tells the person to "Go Fish," and that person chooses one card from the fish pond.

- Continue playing in this fashion, going in a circle until all the cards have been placed into sets of four. The person with the most sets is the winner.

Stamped Garden Markers

Brighten up your garden with stamped markers that identify all the different vegetables, flowers, and herbs growing around your home. These are quick to make and would also be a lovely gift for anyone with a green thumb.

Let's Make It

Measurement: Approximately 3½" x 1"   ●   **Time:** ½ hour

MATERIALS

- Wax paper
- Oven-bake polymer clay (we are using Sculpey III—a 2-oz. block makes four markers)
- 2 chopsticks or ¼ dowels
- Small rolling pin
- Butter knife
- Alphabet rubber stamps with ¼" letters
- Baking parchment paper
- Cookie sheet
- Oven

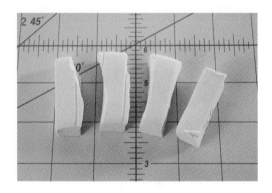

CONDITION THE CLAY

1. Set out one place mat-sized piece of wax paper on your work surface for each person.

2. Break a 2-oz. block of oven-bake clay into four pieces.

3. Take one piece of clay and work it with your hands a bit, rolling it into a log shape. (Polymer clay is firmer than traditional modeling clay, but the warmth from your hands will soften it just enough for rolling.)

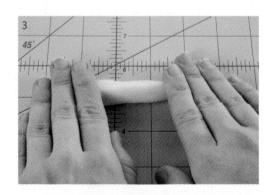

52

MAKE THE GARDEN MARKERS

④ Set the chopsticks on your work surface so that they are parallel and positioned a little more than 1" apart.

⑤ Place the conditioned clay in between the top end of the chopsticks.

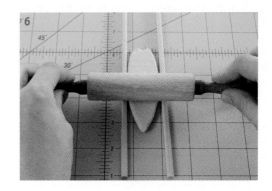

⑥ Slowly roll out the clay, using the chopsticks as a level guide for the rolling pin. (This step will help you create an even slab of clay, which will help it bake evenly.)

⑦ You will know when the slab is level because the rolling pin will glide easily across the chopsticks. It should end up being about 3½"–4" long.

⑧ Set the chopsticks aside and use a butter knife to trim the marker. Even out the sides so it is about 1" wide. Cut a point (about ½") at one end of the marker. Square off the top of each marker and gently round the corners with your fingers, if you like.

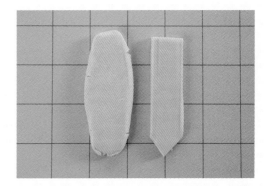

⑨ Use the alphabet rubber stamps to "write" the names of your vegetables, herbs, or flowers vertically on each marker. It is helpful to make a list of these names beforehand to clarify spelling for everyone.

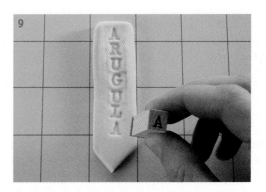

⑩ Place the markers on a parchment-lined cookie sheet and bake according to the manufacturer's instructions. They will shrink slightly and harden quite a bit.

⑪ Allow the markers to cool completely before placing them in your garden.

⑫ These make a great gift. Bundle up a bunch of garden markers with a ribbon to present with a wildflower gift garden (Chapter 7).

Kid-Sized Garden Gnome

arden gnomes are treasured helpers thought to bring luck to your home and garden. Kids will get a kick out of personalizing these life-sized gnomes and can even create a series of mythical gnome friends to swap out throughout the seasons.

Let's Make It

Measurement: 33" tall ● **Time:** 1–2 hours

1

MATERIALS

- 33" tomato cage (with three legs and three rings)
- Duct tape (1 roll each of blue, red, white, black, silver, and flesh tones)
- Old sheet, curtain, or about 2 yards of plain fabric
- Pencil
- Scissors
- Straight pins

MAKE THE GNOME'S LINING

1. Turn the tomato cage upside down and hold the three legs together to create the basic gnome shape. Duct-tape the tops of the legs together, covering all sharp points.

2. Place the tomato cage on its side on the fabric, lining up the tip with a corner and the side of the form extending down one edge.

3. Keep one hand on the tip of the tomato cage so it remains in the corner, and then roll it in the fabric to create a pattern piece.

4. Pencil a line where the bottom ring of the cage grazes the fabric in an arc shape similar to a slice of pie. (Refer to the illustration.)

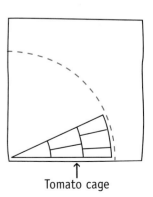

Tomato cage

⑤ Cut out the fabric on the line to create what will become the lining of the gnome.

⑥ Wrap the lining snugly around the gnome and pin it in place in a straight line from top to bottom.

⑦ Trim away any excess fabric along the edge and bottom of the gnome.

⑧ On a piece of scrap paper, draw a sketch of how your finished gnome should appear. Traditional gnomes have white hair, wear red hats, and are dressed in tunics in historic colors such as blue or green. Many have beards, and some even carry garden tools such as a shovel. That said, have fun with it and dress your garden gnome any way you like.

⑨ With the fabric still on the tomato cage, pencil in general lines on the fabric where the different duct tapes will be placed.

⑩ Remove the pins and lay the gnome lining flat on the floor.

⑪ Go over any faint lines so your design is clearly visible.

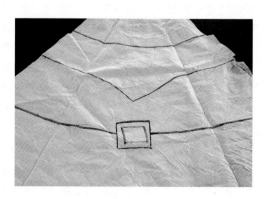

DRESS YOUR GNOME

12 Working one color at a time, stick strips of duct tape directly onto the lining fabric. Fill in the general sections first. Overlap the strips slightly as you go and smooth out any rough edges.

13 Place a small circle of flesh-toned duct tape in the middle of the white hair and beard section to create a face.

14 Add small blue or black circles for eyes.

15 To create the belt, first make a band of black duct tape. Center a large square of silver duct tape along the belt, and then place a smaller square of the black tape inside the silver to give the illusion of a buckle.

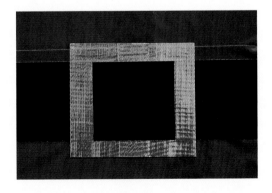

16 Use scissors to trim any excess tape from the bottom
edge of the lining.

17 Wrap the gnome material around the tomato cage
and apply coordinating-colored duct tape to secure
it closed down the entire back seam.

TIP

These gnomes can be removed from the
tomato cage for easy storage.

You can also create several different
gnomes or even an entire gnome wardrobe
to swap out throughout the year.

Marbled Paper

Create some amazing marbled paper using kid-friendly items from around the house. Let your kids get messy and then watch their faces light up as they see their prints develop. Use these prints for other projects in this book to create one-of-a-kind paper goods. Or better yet, frame a series by your budding artist to display in your home.

Let's Make It

Time: 15 minutes (or as long as you like)

MATERIALS
- Cookie sheets
- Kitchen towels
- Baby shampoo
- Tempera or acrylic paints
- Plain paper (watercolor paper works especially well)
- Paper towels

CREATE THE MARBLED PAPER

1 Place a cookie sheet on top of a kitchen towel in front of each of your little artists.

2 Squirt 1–2 tablespoons of shampoo onto each cookie sheet. Add a bit of water and rub it around vigorously in the cookie sheet to create a thick, foamy lather.

3 You can add shampoo or water as needed so that enough foam is created to cover the bottom of the tray. Then smooth out the foam with your hands.

4　Wash your hands before the next step. What's great about using baby shampoo for this project is that it is not heavily perfumed, will not sting if the children accidentally rub their eyes, and it makes washing up a breeze.

5　Add a few drops of paint to the foamy layer. If you like, add a few different colors and discover how the different colors blend.

6　Draw the paint around in the foam using fingers, or something pointy such as a chopstick, fork, skewer, or toothpick.

7　Place a sheet of plain paper on top of the colorful foam and gently rub the paper across the surface of the foam. Experiment with applying different amounts of pressure to see what your results will be.

8　Carefully lift the paper at one corner, removing it from the foam. You will see waves of colorful foam creating a marbled design all over the surface of the paper. Allow to dry.

9　If there is any remaining foam, place each print face down on a paper towel and gently rub the back of the print.

10　Allow each print to dry completely before displaying or using in other projects.

Stained-Glass Butterflies

Create a bevy of butterflies with wings reminiscent of stained glass. Using a simple technique you may recall from your own childhood, your kids will enjoy bringing these fluttery friends to life and setting them free to fly throughout your home.

Let's Make It

Measurement: approximately 6" x 6" • **Time:** ½ hour

MATERIALS
- Newspaper
- ¾" x 6" wood craft sticks (similar to tongue depressors)
- Acrylic paints and paintbrushes
- Old wax crayons in different colors
- Box grater

- Protective cloth (such as an old dish towel)
- Wax paper
- Pressing cloth (an old t-shirt works great)
- Iron
- Scissors
- Craft glue

PAINT THE BUTTERFLY BODIES
1. Place newspaper on your work surface.
2. Paint one side each of two craft sticks for each butterfly being created. Allow to dry.

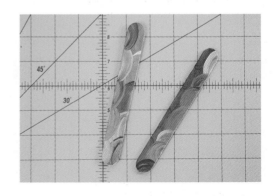

MAKE THE "STAINED-GLASS" WINGS

❸ Work with your kids to carefully create a small pile of crayon shavings using the box grater. (When choosing a color palette, consider how colors will blend as the wax melts.)

❹ Place a protective cloth onto your ironing board. Place a piece of wax paper (about 12" x 12") on top of the protective cloth.

❺ Cover the wax paper with a thin layer of crayon shavings, leaving a border of about ½".

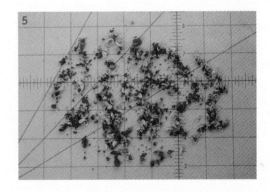

❻ Place another piece of wax paper on top of the first, keeping the crayon shavings in between.

❼ Put the pressing cloth on top of this wax paper and crayon sandwich. Press lightly with a low iron on a dry setting (no steam) for just a few moments until the crayon shavings melt between the wax paper sheets.

❽ Remove the pressing cloth and allow the "stained glass" to cool completely.

❾ Cut a freeform butterfly-wing shape out of each "stained-glass" wax sheet.

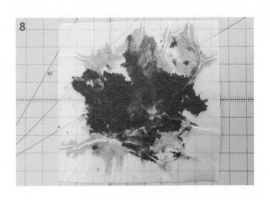

ASSEMBLE THE BUTTERFLIES

⑩ Run a line of glue down the back of one of the painted craft sticks.

⑪ Center a set of wings on the stick and glue in place. Repeat with another painted stick, sandwiching the wings in between them. Allow the glue to dry.

⑫ Set the butterflies free around your home by taping them to window frames, or hanging them in groups using invisible thread or fishing wire.

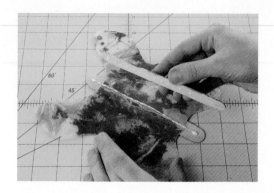

Nothing is better on a hot day than something cold and sweet. Whip up a batch of shaved ice made from your favorite citrus fruits and serve it up to your friends and family in adorable citrus cups. This cool summery treat will quickly become a refreshing favorite on hot summer days.

Let's Make It

Measurement: Individual serving-sized ● **Time:** About 3 hours

MATERIALS

- 8 citrus fruits such as lemons, limes, oranges, and grapefruits (it's fun to experiment with different combinations—our recent favorite is 6 lemons and 2 oranges)

- Knife

- Mesh strainer

- Large measuring cup (6-cup is great)

- Citrus reamer

- Water

- Spoon or rubber spatula

- Sugar

- Muffin tin or cookie sheet

- Freezer

- Baking pan (13" x 9" works perfectly)

- Fork

MAKE THE CITRUS MIXTURE

❶ Cut each of the fruits in half.

❷ Place the mesh strainer on top of the measuring cup.

❸ Hold half of a fruit in one hand and the reamer in the other. Place the pointy end of the citrus reamer into the fruit and twist it around in the fruit. The pulp and seeds will go into the strainer as the juice drips into the measuring cup.

❹ Set each citrus cup aside for now.

❺ Continue in this manner until all of the fruits have been juiced.

6 Use a spoon or rubber spatula to smooth and press the remaining pulp into the mesh strainer to get every last drop of juice into the measuring cup.

7 Determine how much juice you have.

8 Add twice as much cold water as there is juice and taste the mixture. It will be very tart, but if it seems too strong, you can add more water.

9 Add sugar to the mixture one tablespoon at a time and stir until it dissolves. Taste it (this is part of the fun) and then add more sugar until the kids decide it is just right.

FREEZE THE CITRUS CUPS

10 Use a spoon to scoop out the remaining pulp from each of the fruit halves.

11. Create a flat bottom on each cup by carefully cutting off a small bit of the end.

12. Place the citrus cups in a muffin tin or on a cookie sheet, and then put it into the freezer.

MAKE THE CITRUS SNOW

13. Pour the citrus mixture into the baking pan.

14. Clear a space in the freezer large enough for the baking pan. Then place the baking pan in the freezer.

15. After about ½ hour, check the mixture to see if ice crystals have begun to form. If not, close the freezer door and check back in another ½ hour. The real fun begins when you see the ice crystals.

16. When crystals have formed, remove the baking pan from the freezer and rake a fork from one end of the pan to the other, pulling through the mixture to break up the ice crystals. Return the pan to the freezer.

17. Every ½ hour, take the pan out of the freezer and repeatedly rake the fork from end to end through the citrus ice. Break up any larger chunks of the semi-frozen mixture with the back of the fork. You will notice it becoming a harder texture each time.

18. Eventually you will end up scraping into the surface of the mixture, shaving it into tiny crystals that look just like snow. Taste it!

19. When you have a baking pan full of citrus snow, you are ready to serve.

SERVE IT UP

20. Remove the citrus cups from the freezer.

21. Fill each of the cups with the shaved ice and serve with a spoon.

22. If there is any shaved ice left over, scoop it into a resealable container for storage in the freezer.

23. Empty citrus cups can be placed into a freezer bag until ready to use.

24. Fluff the shaved ice with a fork before scooping it out the next time you serve it.

Whimsical Wind Chimes

W hether it's sports or animals, every child has something they absolutely love. In this project, highlight your kids' favorite things by creating a whimsical set of wind chimes. They are sure to enjoy seeing their creations sway and clink together in the breeze.

Let's Make It

Time: 1 hour

MATERIALS

- Scratch paper and pencils
- 8" x 10½" sheets of artist's-grade shrink plastic (such as PolyShrink)
- Sandpaper (320-grit)
- Colored pencils
- Scissors
- Single-hole punch
- Baking parchment paper
- Cookie sheet
- Oven
- Invisible thread or fishing wire

CREATE THE CHIMES

1. Create your designs on scratch paper. Consider that the plastic will shrink by about half, so your images need to be large. Younger children may prefer to use rubber stamps or trace images from books.

2. Sand a sheet of shrink plastic according to the manufacturer's instructions.

3. Cut a strip of sanded shrink plastic measuring about 8" x 1½". This will be the top piece of the wind chimes from which the other pieces will dangle.

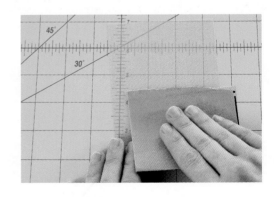

④ Place the sanded shrink plastic on top of the designs and trace each with a pencil.

⑤ Use colored pencils to add color to each of the designs as well as the top piece.

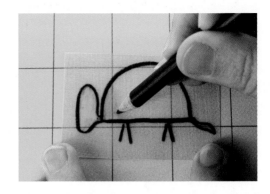

⑥ Cut out the designs with scissors.

⑦ Punch a hole in the top of each design.

⑧ Punch evenly spaced holes across the top piece according to how many designs have been made.

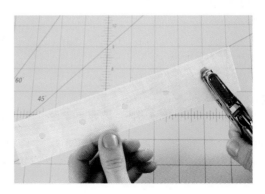

SHRINK THE CHIMES

9 Space the plastic pieces on a cookie sheet lined with parchment paper.

10 Bake according to manufacturer's instructions. This is a quick process and really fun to watch through the oven door.

11 Remove the cookie sheet from the oven and allow the pieces to cool completely.

Before   After

STRING UP THE CHIMES

12 Use invisible thread or fishing wire to dangle the chimes from the top strip and hang them by a breezy window.

D ive in to a big bowl of buttons and use them to create a permanent tribute to your favorite flowers. Head to the garden for inspiration and make a darling illustration to remind you of summer blossoms.

Let's Make It

Time: 1 hour

MATERIALS

- Scrap paper and crayons, markers, or colored pencils

- Buttons in a variety of colors and sizes

- Glue

- Pre-stretched artist's canvas (we are using 5" x 5", but you can make these in any size you like)

- Acrylic paints and paintbrushes

CREATE SOMETHING SPECIAL

1. Sketch the general image of your flower(s) onto scratch paper and indicate the colors.

2. Sort through your buttons and choose ones that will fit your design. Place them onto the sketch so you have a visual of how the finished piece will appear.

3. Paint the flower stems directly onto your canvas using acrylic paints. Use the sketch as a guide for placement.

4. Glue the buttons onto the canvas one at a time, using your sketch as a guide.

5. Allow to dry before displaying.

CHAPTER 4

Back to School

A big thrill in fall is the beginning of school. Kids are eager and excited about all that is possible in the year ahead. This chapter features a variety of craft projects to help reinforce what your children are learning at school through hands-on play. You can tailor each of these projects to address and evolve with your child's individual needs. Each has been designed to be both fun and educational—from the creative process through to the finished pieces.

Alphabet Beanbag Toss

Kids young and old appreciate a good beanbag toss game. Instead of buying one, how about making your own? You and your kids can whip up this alphabetical version in a few hours using inexpensive materials. And when the fun of making is done, you will be amazed how many ways your kiddos will interpret this game.

Let's Make It

Measurement: 30" x 18" • **Time:** 1–2 hours

MATERIALS

- 1 piece of duck cloth or heavyweight cotton canvas measuring 60" x 18"

NOTE: You can have yardage cut at the fabric store, or simply cut a piece from a cotton painter's drop cloth.

- Duct tape in a variety of colors
- Scissors
- Pencil
- Letter stencils measuring approx. 2½" high

NOTE: You can easily make your own by printing an uppercase/lowercase alphabet. (For example: We used Tahoma font at size 250.)

- Paint brushes
- Fabric paint
- Dried beans, lentils, or rice

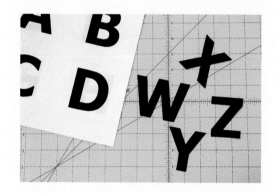

MAKE THE ALPHABET MAT

1. Cut the duck cloth in half so that you have two pieces, each measuring 30" x 18".

2. Use lengths of duct tape to bind the mat by wrapping it over all of the edges.

3. Lay out the letter stencils evenly on the mat. It may help to tape them in place while you are doing this step.

4. Lightly pencil around each of the stencils.

5. Paint in each of the letters using fabric paint, following the manufacturer's instructions as to how to apply the paint.

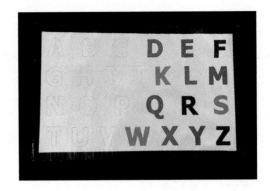

MAKE THE BEANBAGS

6. Cut out twelve 4" squares from the other piece of duck cloth you set aside earlier.

7. Put two of the squares of together and bind them on three sides using the duct tape to create a pouch. Make six all together, binding three with one color duct tape and three with another color duct tape.

8. Place some dried beans/lentils into the open end of each pouch. Seal the fourth side closed with duct tape and you're done!

Let's Play

- Take turns throwing a beanbag onto the mat. Come up with a list of words that start with that letter and then compare lists.

- Try that same game, but this time brainstorming lists of words that end with the target letters. Or have both teams throw a bean bag and then list words that include both letters.

- Make a larger version of the mat and play a kinesthetic team game similar to "twister". Write words with a given number of letters onto cards and toss them into a hat. Teams take turns spelling with their hands and feet.

ABC Collage Book

What better way to reinforce the alphabet and its accompanying sounds than by making a game of it. Your kids will create a personalized alphabet book at their own developmental level, which they can enjoy and expand on as their reading abilities progress. The goal is to heighten awareness of letter sounds, with the child initiating conversations that serve as a bridge to reading activities.

Let's Make It

Measurement: 5½" x 8½" • **Time:** 1 hour (to get started)

MATERIALS

- 14 pieces of 8½" x 11" white paper
- 1 piece of 8½" x 11" cardstock for the cover
- Cardboard box (such as a shoebox)
- Stapler

- Spoon
- Scissors, glue, old magazines and catalogs, colored pencils, crayons, markers, etc.

MAKE A SIMPLE PAMPHLET-STYLE BOOK

1. Fold each piece of paper and cardstock in half, short end to short end, creasing on the fold.

2. Slip the folded papers one inside the other to form a folded leaflet-style book with 28 pages. Then slip the book inside the folded cover.

3 Place the cardboard box on the floor with the flat side facing up as your work surface. Open the book and flatten it with the inner side facing down on top of the box, being sure to keep the pages lined up.

4 Open the stapler and press three evenly spaced staples through the entire spine of the book right into the cardboard box.

5 Carefully pull the book from the cardboard box and turn it over so you can see the sharp ends of the staples inside the book. Use a spoon to press the staples closed.

PERSONALIZE THE ABC BOOK WITH COLLAGE

6 Write the title on the first page of the book.

7 Open to the next page so you are looking at a two-page spread. Use a pencil to label the left page with an upper- and lowercase "Aa". Turn to the next two-page spread and continue labeling each upper-left page with upper- and lowercase letters until the book is filled.

8 Have your kids cut out upper- and lowercase letters from old magazines, catalogs and newspapers, then glue them on top of the penciled-in letters on corresponding pages.

MAKE IT A TREASURE HUNT

9 Look for images to put in the book, trying to represent as many sounds as possible. Talk about individual letters and the different sounds they make. Glue them to the appropriate pages as new words come up. This is a great project to spread out over time—dedicate some special time each day to work on this book together.

F elt boards evoke such peaceful imaginary play for young children. In this project, you and your kids will combine a few basic materials to create a fully stocked felt board that will strengthen their increasing vocabulary as well as offer hours of entertainment.

Let's Make It

Measurement: 8" x 10" ● **Time:** ½ hour

MATERIALS

- 1 piece of felt measuring about 12" x 14" to cover the canvas
- 8" x 10" stretched artist's canvas
- Staple gun or duct tape
- Felt scraps in a variety of colors

- Scissors
- Blank index cards or cardstock
- Pen or marker

MAKE THE FELT BOARD

1. Place the 12" x 14" felt on a sturdy surface such as the counter or floor. Place the canvas face down, centering it on the felt.

2. Wrap the felt up over the sides, starting at the center of opposing sides.

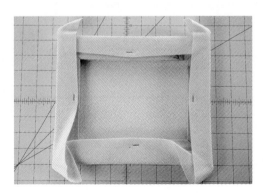

3 Pull the felt tightly as you secure it to the back of the frame using a staple gun or duct tape.

MAKE ALL THE TRIMMINGS

4 Cut out a variety of basic shapes from the felt scraps such as circles, squares, stars, rectangles, triangles, hexagons, etc. If possible, cut one of each shape out of several different colors of felt.

5 Write each of the shape names and color names on a card. Then, write each of numbers 1–10 on a card. (For the cards, we simply quartered blank 4" x 6" index cards.)

6 When not in use, all of the felt pieces and cards can easily be stored in a large envelope or shoebox.

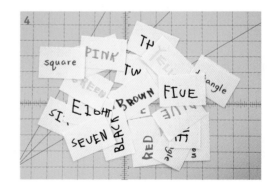

Let's Play

- Start by having the child select a card or two and then find those pieces to put on the felt board (for example: purple octagon).

- As the child gets the hang of it, the game can evolve (for example: four circles).

A Few More Ideas and Inspiration

You can make this activity as simple or complex as you like. Start with a basic set of colors and shapes. Let the child play with the felt pieces to create animals and other things from their imagination. As they illustrate new vocabulary, write those words on new cards and review them together.

I once "caught" my daughter cutting up bits of extra felt into arcs and tiny dots in order to create a smiling tree on her felt board—it was awesome! Be sure to keep extra materials accessible for your children to encourage their ownership of this project.

A great way to reinforce what your kids are creating is to take photographs of what they make (for example: an underwater scene with fish made entirely by using these simple shapes)—you can print the picture and put it on a card for future reference, hang it on the wall, or print a series to create their own original books.

Flashcards to Go

Vocabulary words do not have to be restricted to a word wall. This project encourages kids to grab a few to go, keeping them right at their fingertips on a handy ring. The cards can easily slip out to play a classic game of concentration whenever they want. And they're not just for vocabulary words—your kids will find about a million ways to use and reuse these felt cards.

Let's Make It

Measurement: 3¼" x 7" • **Time:** 1 hour

MATERIALS

- For each card, you will need:

  1 piece of thick felt measuring 4" x 7"
  1 "bottom" fabric piece measuring 3" x 4"
  1 "top" fabric piece measuring 5¼" x 4"

- Straight pins
- Needle and thread (or a sewing machine)

- Pinking shears (optional)
- ⅜" grommets and grommet pliers
- 3" x 5" index cards
- Scissors, glue, old magazines and catalogs, colored pencils, crayons, markers, etc.
- Metal book ring or carabiner

TIP

Sewing: Simplified

This project presents a great opportunity to teach your kids a few basic sewing techniques. Work hand-over-hand with your child stitching a large-eyed needle threaded with yarn through an open weave fabric such as burlap. You will be surprised how quickly your child picks it up.

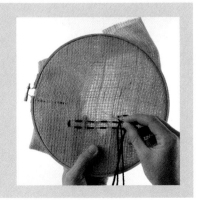

ASSEMBLE THE CARDS

1 Fold each of the fabric pieces in half by bringing one 4" edge atop the other 4" edge with right side of the fabric facing out.

2 Slip a folded "top" and "bottom" fabric piece onto either of the 4" ends of each felt piece and pin in place.

3 Using needle and thread (or sewing machine), stitch the entire perimeter of the piece using about a ¼" seam allowance, fastening the fabric to the felt in a manner that creates a flap at either end.

4 Stitch a straight line across the fabric 1¼" down from the top fabric's edge.

5 To prevent fraying, use pinking shears to trim the long sides.

6 Following the manufacturer's instructions in the grommet kit, place a grommet in one of the top corners of each felt card.

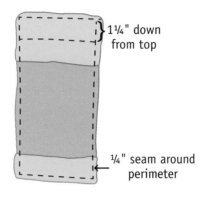

1¼" down from top

¼" seam around perimeter

FINISH THE FLASHCARDS

7 Slip a blank index card under both flaps on one side of the felt flashcard to help you visualize the area that will be in view on each card. Pencil in a template if needed.

8 Each felt flashcard has two sides—have your kids write the word on one index card, and then draw or glue an image of the word on another card. Use old magazines, catalogs, etc. to find coordinating images.

9 Once you have created a set of flashcards, simply slip a book ring or carabiner through the grommets, and your kiddo is good to go.

giraffe

Lift-a-Flap Story Book

Kids will love creating their very own books with lift-a-flap pages that reveal hidden pictures. Start small with just a page or two and talk about how the sequence of the story could progress in the future. Add more pages later to develop the story further. It can be our secret that this project is a great way to introduce and reinforce new vocabulary.

Let's Make It

Measurement: 8½" x 5½" ● **Time:** ½ hour per page

MATERIALS

- 1 piece of 8½" x 11" cardstock (per page)
- Ruler
- Pencil
- Single hole punch

- Craft knife and self-healing mat (optional)
- Scissors, glue, old magazines and catalogs, colored pencils, crayons, markers, etc.
- Three metal book rings

PREPARE THE PAGES

1. Fold each piece of cardstock in half, short end to short end, creasing on the fold.

2. Look at a page in landscape/wide position with the fold at the top. Using the ruler as a guide, mark three spots ½" from the bottom edge indicating where you will punch the holes: 1" in from the left, 1" in from the right, and center 4¼" in from either side.

3. Once you have all pages marked, punch the holes through both layers on each page.

3

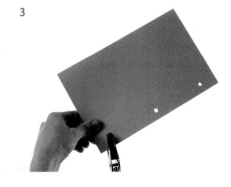

SELECT IMAGES

4 Have your kids draw or search through magazines and catalogs to cut out images corresponding to a few words from a current vocabulary list. Images should measure approximately 2" x 3".

5 As you both work to gather images, create a short story that incorporates 2–3 of the vocabulary words in each sentence. Write a draft of the story on scratch paper.

PREPARE AND CUT THE LIFT-A-FLAPS

6 Write out the first sentence of the story on a folded page (fold is on the bottom and holes on the top). In the spots where a vocabulary word will go, do not write the word at this time—instead, place the image and lightly pencil around it to indicate the size needed for the flap. Repeat for additional images on the page.

7 Set the images for that page aside and lightly outline both sides and the bottom of a rectangle where the image was.

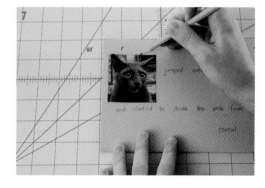

8 Unfold the page and use a craft knife and self-healing mat to cut three sides of each rectangle you just drew, creating the flaps. Open each flap, creasing on the fold.

FINISH THE BOOK

9 Fold each page back together and lift each flap to reveal the area on the page underneath. Glue the images to their corresponding hidden spots each page.

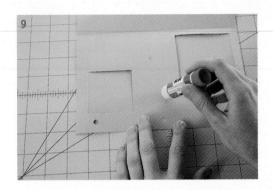

10 When all images for a page are glued in place, open the page and look on the underside framework around the flaps. Apply glue to that framework and press the page together keeping the flaps open. Allow each page to dry with the flaps open.

11 When dry, write the corresponding vocabulary words under each flap.

12 Your kids can decorate each page as much as they like.

13 Gather the pages, hook them together with book rings, and enjoy reading your lift-a-flap story book.

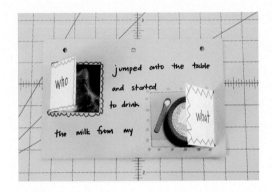

Local Leaves Memory Game

What better way to familiarize yourselves with local foliage than by sourcing your surroundings to whip up a classic memory game. Collect leaves during various seasons to expand this activity throughout the year by comparing colors and textures.

Let's Make It

Measurement: 5" x 8" ● **Time:** ½ hour

MATERIALS
- A variety of leaves
- An old hardcover book for pressing leaves
- 5" x 8" index cards
- Mod Podge
- Foam paint brushes
- Colored pencils, crayons, markers, etc.

HEAD OUTSIDE
1. Collect a bunch of leaves from your yard or a nearby park.
2. Press the leaves in a book for a few days.
3. Apply a thin coat of Mod Podge to the card before placing down the leaf. Apply another coat on top of the leaf and card and allow it to dry. Once dry, apply a second coat.
4. Write the name of each leaf on another card.
5. When finished, your kids can mix up the cards to play memory. For an added challenge, create one card with the leaf, one with the written name of the leaf, and one with a photo of the tree.

CHAPTER 5

Winter Wonderland

Celebrate winter by creating toys, games, and decorations inspired by falling snow and the chill in the air. From playing with your food to a one-of-a-kind stuffed snowman, this chapter has something for everyone and is filled with projects that are certain to brighten any winter's day.

Snowball Fight Wreath

Dress up your front door with a ring of whimsical white snowballs that doubles as target practice. This project is simple to make and is sure to keep everyone smiling all winter long, even when it's not in play.

Let's Make It

Measurement: 12"–14" in diameter ● **Time:** 1–2 hours

MATERIALS
- 12" wreath form
- White felt (or any white fabric) about 1 yard
- Low-temp hot glue gun
- Sticky-backed 1"-wide hook and loop strips
- Newspaper
- White acrylic paints
- Foam paintbrush

PREPARE THE WREATH FORM
1. Wrap the wreath form using strips of the white felt and use a small amount of hot glue to secure them in place.
2. Apply the soft-sided sticky-backed hook and loop strips in bands around one side of the wreath form.

MAKE THE SNOWBALLS

3. Place a dropcloth on your work surface.

4. Spread out single sheets of newspaper.

5. Mix a semi-opaque white color wash by diluting two parts of white acrylic paint with one part of water in an empty jar. Stir to mix.

6. Use the paintbrush to apply the white color wash to the newspaper, covering each sheet entirely to the edge but not saturating the paper.

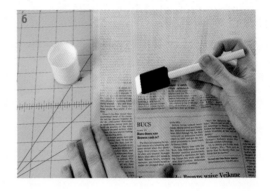

7. Allow the painted pages to dry completely. If possible, leave them in a sunny spot to speed up the drying process.

8. Ball up each sheet of the painted newspaper in your hands, trying not to compress it.

9. Cut out 1"–2" circles from the white felt. You will need one felt circle for each snowball.

10. Cut 1" squares from the scratchy-sided sticky-backed hook and loop strips. Apply one to each felt circle.

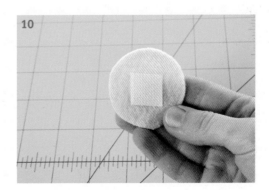

⑪ Use some hot glue to apply one of these felt circles to the back of each snowball.

⑫ Arrange the snowballs on the wreath form using the hook and loop strips.

Let's Play

Hold the wreath while your kids throw the snowballs through it as target practice.

When your kids aren't working on their technique, simply reattach the snowballs to the wreath.

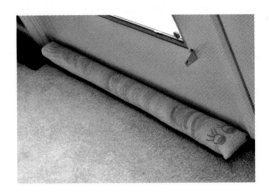

Protect your home from chilly air sneaking in around windows and under doorways by creating these draft snakes featuring your child's artwork. In this project, you will work together to make keepsakes that are both fun and functional.

Let's Make It

Time: ½–1 hour

MATERIALS

- Tape measure
- ½ yard of linen or cotton fabric
- Scissors
- White paper
- Tape
- Fabric crayons
- Iron
- Needle and thread (or a sewing machine)
- Rice (or other weighted material for stuffing)

CREATE THE DRAFT SNAKES

1. Have kids go through their original artwork to select a few pieces for transfer, or they can start sketching new designs.

2. Measure the width of the doorway or window for which you are creating this draft snake.

3. Cut a 6"-wide piece of your fabric so that the length is 2" longer than the width of your doorway or window.

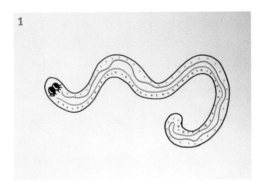

1

4. Follow the manufacturer's instructions for your particular brand of fabric crayons to create and transfer your child's drawing to the fabric. (The product we used says to draw images onto white paper, and then transfer the images to fabric using an iron.)

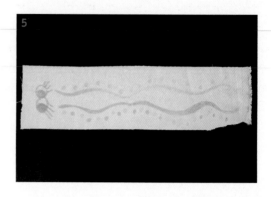

5. Fold the fabric right sides together the entire length of the draft snake.

6. Use a needle and thread (or sewing machine) to stitch around three sides of the fabric, leaving one end open for turning.

7. Turn the piece right side out.

8. Fill the piece with rice or other weighted material. Use a cardboard toilet paper or paper towel tube as a funnel.

9. Hand-stitch the end closed.

10. Give your snake a little shake to evenly distribute the filling and place it in your drafty doorway or window.

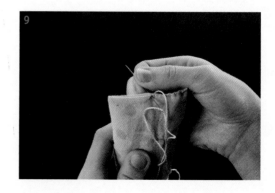

Kids love paper crafts, and in this project we combine two of the classics. Snowflake pinwheels are fun, simple to make, and even teach a few lessons on geometry and engineering without anyone noticing.

Let's Make It

Measurement: 4"–5" ● **Time:** ½ hour

MATERIALS

- White paper cut into 4"–5" squares
- Scissors
- Ruler
- Pencil
- Pushpins
- Small beads
- Wooden chopsticks (or small dowels)

MAKE THE SNOWFLAKES

1. Fold one of the paper squares in half, and then in half again.

2. Cut into the folded paper along the edges, folds, and corners.

3. Unfold the paper to reveal your snowflake.

MAKE THE PINWHEEL

④ Get another one of the paper squares.

⑤ Use a ruler to draw a light pencil line from corner to corner on both diagonals.

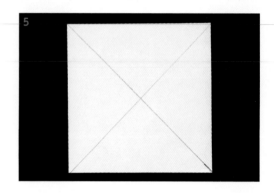

⑥ Cut down just slightly more than halfway to the center along one of the diagonal lines.

⑦ Repeat for all four corners.

⑧ Take one of the pushpins and pierce the corner tip of one of the triangles.

⑨ Repeat on the other three sides of the square, piercing the corner tip in the same spot as you did with the first.

10. Pierce the pin through the center X on the square, creating a pinwheel.

11. Use that same pin to pierce the center of the snowflake.

12. Place a small bead on the pin as a spacer.

13. Press the fully loaded pushpin all the way into the end of the chopstick or dowel.

14. Gently spin the snowflake and pinwheel a few times on the nail to open the holes ever so slightly.

15. Hold the chopstick, blow into the pinwheel, and watch the snowflakes spin.

Birdseed Garland

String some tasty snacks for your feathered
friends that stick around in the winter and
enjoy watching them visit for birdseed. As the seed
disappears, the birds can make use of the garland
materials to reinforce their nests.

Let's Make It

Measurement: 3' lengths ● **Time:** ½–1 hour

MATERIALS

- Birdseed
- 1–2 jars of peanut butter (or any nut butter
  alternative)
- Medium pine cones
- Garden twine or string
- Cheesecloth cut into 8" squares

MAKE THE PINECONE SNACKS

1. Spread out an old tablecloth on your work surface.
2. Pour some of the birdseed into a large bowl.
3. Spread peanut butter into all the nooks and crannies
   of the pine cones. Kids love getting their hands
   sticky doing this.

4. Roll each pine cone in the birdseed, pressing it into the peanut butter until well coated.

5. Tie some twine around the top of each seed-filled pine cone. Make a knot.

MAKE THE SEED BUNDLES

6. Take a tablespoon of peanut butter and roll it in the birdseed, kneading it until it has been thoroughly packed with birdseed.

7. Place the peanut butter birdseed ball in the center of each 8" square of cheesecloth and tie it into a bundle using some of the twine.

STRING UP THE GARLAND

8. Lay out a 3' length of the twine.

9. Use the twine ties on the pine cone and seed bundles to attach five of them evenly spaced along the 3' length of twine to create a garland.

10. Take the garlands outside and tie them to the branches of trees around your home.

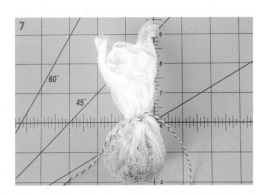

Marshmallow Metropolis

Kids of all ages will agree, one of the best things about winter is hot chocolate. The next time you and your kids are enjoying a cup of warm cocoa, gather a few materials from around the kitchen and start building your own marshmallow town. Encourage your kids to play with their food in this project and join in on the fun.

Let's Make It

Time: Until the marshmallows run out

MATERIALS

- Flat-bottomed paper coffee filters
- Various empty vessels (try using different shapes such as yogurt cups, food storage containers, and empty mugs and bowls)
- 1–2 bags of marshmallows
- Flour or confectioner's sugar

PREPARE THE WORK AREA

1. Spread out an old tablecloth to protect your work surface.
2. Set a small dish with a few tablespoons of water between every few people.
3. Place a paper coffee filter in an empty vessel for building. The filter will absorb water and allow for easy removal of the finished piece when it is dry.

CONSTRUCT THE BUILDINGS

4. Dip a marshmallow into the water to just barely moisten it and then place it in the bottom of the building vessel.

⑤ One marshmallow at a time, fill in the bottom of the vessel by working from the outside in toward the center until the entire base is packed snugly with marshmallows.

⑥ Continue to work up the sides of the vessel, being careful not to use too much water. Once you have worked several levels high, you are done. (The marshmallows should be packed tightly, but not popping out.)

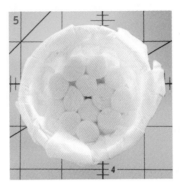 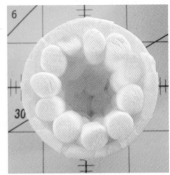

⑦ Sprinkle the marshmallows with a small amount of flour or confectioner's sugar to absorb excess water.

⑧ Allow to dry overnight.

⑨ With the marshmallows still in the coffee filter, remove it from the vessel. Carefully peel back the filter from the sides of the building, but leave it attached on the bottom.

⑩ Allow to dry overnight again.

⑪ Remove the coffee filter from the entire piece and carefully set it right side up.

⑫ Place a group of these marshmallow buildings down the center of a table as a whimsical wintery decoration.

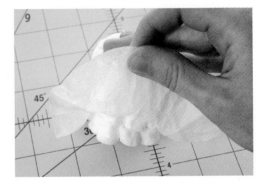

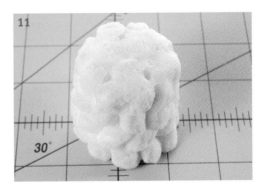

TIP

Make Your Own Marshmallows

Homemade marshmallows are light, delicious, and so simple to make using readily available ingredients—you just need to make them a day or so in advance if using them for this project. Do an online search for "homemade marshmallows" to find a recipe and make some marshmallows from scratch. A benefit of making your own is that you can cut them into blocks, strips, or any size/ shape you wish to inspire your little builders.

Snowman Softie

Kids will love snuggling up with their very own handmade stuffed snowman. Work together to stitch up a soft pal of their own design. Once they make one, they'll be eager to create all sorts of original soft friends.

Let's Make It

Time: 1 hour

MATERIALS

- ½ yard of white polar fleece
- 3 round plates of different sizes
- Pencil
- Scissors
- Felt scraps
- 3 buttons
- Blunt-tipped embroidery needle
- Embroidery floss in a variety of colors
- Fiberfill stuffing

MAKE YOUR PATTERN

1. Fold the polar fleece in half with right sides together to create a double layer of fabric.

2. Place the largest plate on the fabric and lightly trace around it with a pencil.

3. Place the medium-sized plate on the fabric, overlapping it slightly with the first circle. Lightly trace around the plate with a pencil.

4. Repeat with the smallest plate on the fabric, overlapping it slightly with medium circle.

5. Cut around the perimeter of the snowman.

ASSEMBLE YOUR SNOWMAN

6 Cut out two circles from felt scraps for eyes and an orange triangle for a carrot nose.

7 Take one of the snowman pattern pieces and lay out the eyes, nose, and buttons to determine placement.

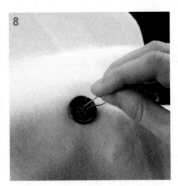

8 Working together with your child using the blunt-tipped embroidery needle and coordinating floss, hand-stitch the eyes, nose, and buttons onto the right side of one of the snowman pattern pieces.

9 Take the two pattern pieces and place them right sides together.

10 Starting at one side of the head, hand-stitch with your child using the blunt-tipped embroidery needle and white floss around the perimeter of the snowman using a ¼"-seam allowance.

11 Leave a 4" opening at the top of the head for turning and stuffing.

12 Reach down inside the opening and turn the snowman right side out.

13 Stuff the snowman through its head with fiberfill until it is firmly packed.

14 Hand-stitch the top of the snowman closed using the white embroidery floss.

15 Kids can make accessories to dress up their softies by cutting scarves from scraps of felt and even adding one of their own infant hats.

CHAPTER 6

Happy Holidays

Holidays provide such great crafting inspiration throughout the year. Using traditional colors and graphics as a springboard, the whimsical craft projects in this chapter highlight these special occasions. And best of all, you can brainstorm with your kids to reinvent each of these designs for other holidays—or just because they are fun.

Glow-in-the-Dark Ghost Wreath

Whip up this spooky ghost for your front door this Halloween. The real fun happens when it gets dark and this ghost shows its true ghoulishly glowing colors. Kids will love getting their hands messy with this project and enjoy endless giggles at their finished creations.

Let's Make It

Measurement: Approximately 1' x 2' ● **Time:** ½ hour (plus 1 day of drying time)

MATERIALS

- 3 yards of 100% cotton cheesecloth
- Scissors
- Glow-in-the-Dark Mod Podge (8-oz. jar)
- 12" wreath form
- Black felt (or other thick black fabric)

MAKE THE GHOST

1. Spread out an old tablecloth to protect your work surface.
2. Cut four 2' lengths of the cheesecloth.
3. Pour about ½ of the Mod Podge into a medium bowl or old plastic container.
4. Dip a piece of cheesecloth into the bowl and stir it around to thoroughly saturate it with the Mod Podge. (Kids will love this part.)
5. Carefully remove the cheesecloth from the bowl and squeeze as much of the Mod Podge as possible from the fabric and back into the bowl for reuse.

6. Hold the wreath form out so your kids can drape the sticky cheesecloth over the top, pulling the corners to open up the fabric all the way and make pointy ends.

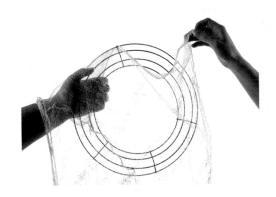

7. Repeat with the other three pieces of cheesecloth, draping them one on top of the other and pulling the ends to form spikes at the bottom.

8. Hang the wreath form on a nail so the ghost can dry completely overnight.

9. Cut out two round eyes and a long oval mouth from the black felt.

10. Adhere the eyes and mouth to the ghost using some of the Mod Podge or craft glue and allow to dry completely before hanging up for display.

Flying Ghouls and Bats

Spooky Halloween decorations are a sure hit with kids. In this project, you will create homemade ghoul and bat forms and use the same technique as in the ghost wreath project to make these dangling creatures to hang outside your house this Halloween.

Let's Make It

Measurement: Makes nine 6" ghouls and/or bats • **Time:** ½ hour (plus 1 day of drying time)

MATERIALS

- 3 yards of 100% cotton cheesecloth
- Scissors
- Newspaper
- Plastic wrap
- 9 empty plastic bottles and cups
- Duct tape
- Twigs
- Mod Podge
- Black spray paint
- Black permanent marker
- Invisible thread or fishing wire

PREPARE YOUR MATERIALS

1. Spread out an old tablecloth to protect your work surface.

2. Cut nine 1' lengths of the cheesecloth.

3. Crush sheets of newspaper into nine balls and cover each with plastic wrap.

4. Secure the balls to the tops of the empty plastic bottles and cups with duct tape.

5. Attach twigs to either side of a few of these to create bat forms.

4

5

MAKE THE GHOULS AND BATS

6 Pour the Mod Podge into a medium bowl or old plastic container.

7 Dip a piece of cheesecloth into the bowl and thoroughly saturate it with the Mod Podge. (Let your kids do this part—they love to get messy, and you can keep your hands clean.)

8 Carefully remove the cheesecloth from the bowl and squeeze as much of the Mod Podge as possible from the fabric and back into the bowl for reuse.

9 Pull the corners of the cheesecloth to open it and drape it over one of the ghoul/bat forms (a and b).

10 Repeat with the remaining eight pieces of cheesecloth and ghoul/bat forms.

11 Allow to dry overnight.

12 Remove the forms from inside the dried ghouls and bats.

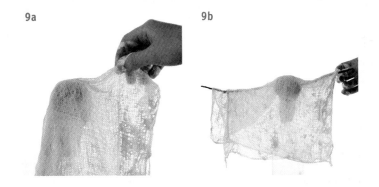

13 Place two small pieces of tape on each bat where you would like them to have eyes.

14 Spray-paint the bats black and allow them to dry. Then remove the tape to reveal the white eyes.

15 Use a black permanent marker to draw eyes on your white ghouls.

16 String up your ghouls and bats using invisible thread and hang your spooky decorations outside for everyone to see.

109

A classic way to play this folded paper game is with colors and numbers, but we are reinterpreting it for a little bit of Halloween fun. Your kids will have a blast coming up with witty one-liners and decorating the game with fun Halloween images.

Let's Make It

Measurement: 4¼" square ● **Time:** ½ hour

MATERIALS
- 1 piece of paper cut to an 8½" square
- Colored pencils, markers, or crayons

FOLD THE PAPER

❶ Fold the square on the diagonal and crease on the fold. Open the paper and repeat the fold for the other diagonal. When done, you will have created an "X" on the paper running from corner to corner.

❷ With the paper open, fold one corner into the center of the X. Crease on the fold. Repeat for the other three corners, folding them into the center and creasing on the folds.

❸ Flip the paper over while keeping those corners folded underneath.

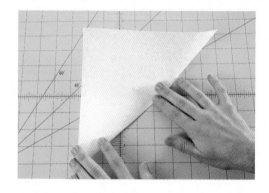

110

4 Fold each of the four corners into the "back" center X one more time. Crease on the folds.

DECORATE THE GAME

5 Decorate each of the four inner flaps with images of spooky friends. You can use the illustrations provided on pages 230–231 in the Appendix, or create your own.

6 Talk about the number of syllables in and spelling of each word as you write the names beside each of the illustrations—this will come into play later.

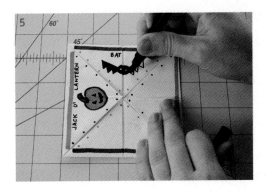

7 Lift each of the four flaps and write a secret message or fortune underneath.

8. Unfold the paper and decorate the four corner squares with more spooky friends.

9. Fold the game up, and you're done!

Let's Play

- With the game folded and your child holding it, have the player choose one of the Halloween friends. Your child says the word and opens and closes the game according to syllable, or with each letter as he or she spells the word out loud. (For example, "frank-en-stein" opens and closes three times.)

- Now the player looks inside the game and chooses another image. The child opens and closes accordingly. Do this step three times so that the player ends up choosing a few of the inner images.

- On the third time through, when the player chooses one of the images, the child lifts up the flap and reveals the secret fortune!

TIP

Create these games for holidays throughout the year and sneak in a little spelling practice while your kids are not looking.

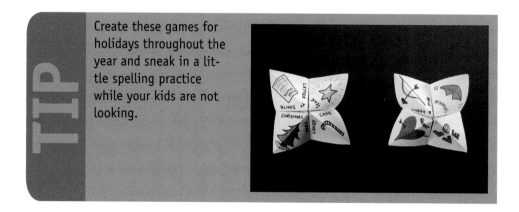

Tisket Tasket Fabric Basket

Weave your own basket for trick-or-treating, egg-collecting, strawberry-picking, or just for fun. Using fabric, glue, and a little bit of rhythm, your kids will create a fun and fully functional woven fabric basket.

Let's Make It

Measurement: Approximately 4" x 4" x 5" ● **Time:** 1 hour

MATERIALS

- Two 18" x 22" pieces of coordinating fabric
- Paper-backed fusible web (such as Wonder Under)
- Iron
- Ruler
- Painter's tape

- Rotary cutter and self-healing mat, or scissors
- Tissue box measuring 4¼" x 4¼" x 5"
- Fabric glue
- 2 yards of medium rick rack (or ribbon)

PREPARE THE FABRIC

1. Fuse your two fabrics together (with the right sides out) following the manufacturer's instructions for the fusible web you are using. You end up with a reversible fabric.

2 With a ruler and pencil, mark 1" increments on the fabric.

3 Cut 1" wide strips of the fused fabric, being sure to cut along the 22" length of the fabric to create 1" wide x 22" long strips.

WEAVE THE BASKET

4 Line up four strips with fabric A facing up.

5 Weave four more strips through them, also with fabric A facing up. Align the weaving so that it is centered both vertically and horizontally.

6 Place the tissue box on top of the weaving.

7 Wrap four strips up one side of the tissue box and tape them to the top of the box.

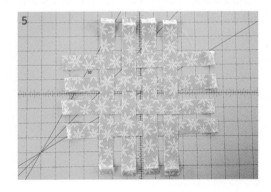

8. Repeat step 7 with the four fabric strips on each side. Tape them snugly to the box top.

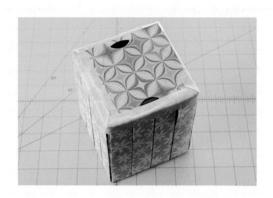

9. Take a strip with fabric B facing up and start at the bottom of one of the sides of the box to weave over and under the strips that are running up the sides of the box.

10. When you have gone all the way around the box and the ends of the fabric strips join, cut the ends so they overlap by about ½".

11. Pull the strip so that it is wrapped snugly around the box. Place a small amount of fabric glue on one end of the strip and tack it to the other end of the strip.

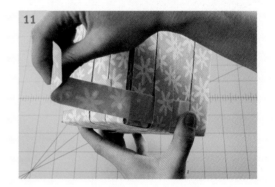

12. Continue to weave four more strips up around the box in the same manner, each time with fabric B facing out.

13. Remove the tape from the strips and very carefully remove the tissue box from inside the woven basket.

14. Tug the ends to tighten up the basket.

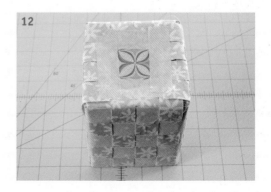

15. Trim the ends of the fabric strips so that each tab measures 1" above the top band of the woven basket.

16. One at a time, fold the tab from the end of a fabric strip over the top of the basket.

17. Use a small amount of fabric glue to secure each of the tabs in place.

18. Repeat steps 16 and 17 until all 16 tabs have been folded over, alternating folding toward the inside and outside of the basket.

FINISH THE BASKET

19. Cut a 12" strip of the fused fabric. This strip will become the handle.

20. Center a 12" length of rick rack on the handle.

21. Glue in place and repeat on the other side of the handle if desired.

22. Glue the ends of the handle to the two opposing sides of the basket.

23. Center rick rack down a 22" fabric strip and glue in place.

24. Glue that fabric strip around the top band of the basket. This will cover the ends of the handles as well as the vertical weaving.

Moody Pumpkinhead

Afavorite activity for kids in fall is carving pumpkins for Halloween. Try something new this year by creating a very special pumpkin character with interchangeable parts. Kids will enjoy switching the facial features as it suits their imagination.

Let's Make It

Time: ½ hour

MATERIALS

- 1 pumpkin
- Sticky-backed hook and loop dots
- Glue
- Scissors
- Felt scraps

PREPARE THE PUMPKIN

1. Wipe your pumpkin with a damp cloth so you have a clean surface.

2. Stick the hook and loop dots onto the pumpkin in the areas where you would like the eyes, nose, ears, and mouth to be placed.

3. Cut out various shapes from felt scraps, and glue them together to create an assortment of whimsical facial features. Stick corresponding hoop and loop dots on the back of the felt shapes.

4. Children will get a kick out of transforming the pumpkin's mood by simply changing the facial features over and over again.

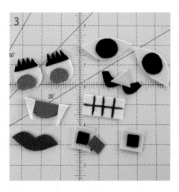

117

Origami Paper Beads

Creating your own handmade paper beads is a great project to do with your kids when you just want to hang out and talk. When you are done, you will have a bowl full of memories, as well as pretty beads to use in other craft projects, jewelry-making, and decorating.

Let's Make It

Measurement: 1" each ● **Time:** ½–1 hour

MATERIALS

- Origami papers (6" squares)
- Ruler
- Pencil or pen
- Craft knife and self-healing mat, or scissors
- Mod Podge
- Small foam brush applicators
- Bamboo skewers

MAKE THE BEADS

1. Draw triangles on your origami papers that taper from 1" wide at the base to a ¼" tip.

2. Use a craft knife on a self-healing mat (or scissors) to cut out all of the triangles.

3. Apply a thin coat of Mod Podge to a 1" section at the wide end of the triangle on the right side of the paper.

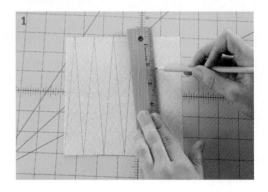

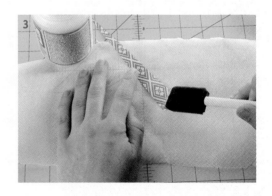

④ Wrap that end around a bamboo skewer with the right side of the paper facing out. The glue you applied to the base will help the paper stick to itself.

⑤ Wiggle the bead to make sure it is not sticking to the skewer.

⑥ With the bead started on the skewer, turn it over and apply a thin coat of the Mod Podge to the entire back side of the origami paper.

⑦ Use your thumb and index finger of one hand to wrap the triangle around itself as you turn the skewer in your other hand. Be sure to keep the paper centered on itself as you wrap.

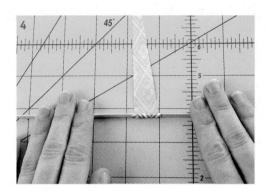

⑧ Carefully wiggle the bead with your fingers to loosen it from the skewer and slip it onto a new skewer for drying. Rest each end of the skewer on a glass so that the beads are not touching anything and allow them to dry.

⑨ Brush a thin topcoat of the Mod Podge on the dried beads to seal and harden them. (Try using Glitter or Glow-in-the-Dark Mod Podge for some extra fun.)

⑩ Allow the beads to dry before using them in other crafts such as jewelry-making.

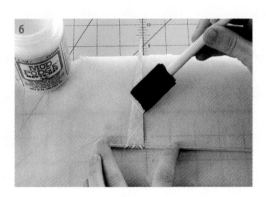

⑪ You can increase or decrease the size of these beads by simply changing the base width when making the paper triangles.

TIP

Recycled Paper Beads

Try making these beads using pages from an old magazine or catalog instead of the origami papers.

As you select pages to use, consider color and graphics when cutting the triangles.

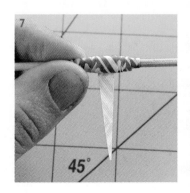

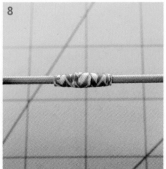

Thanksgiving is a special time to celebrate with family and friends and express gratitude for all the good things in our lives. We use classic hand turkeys as a springboard for this project and transform them into keepsake place cards for your holiday table. Kids will enjoy making these as well as sharing in the Thanksgiving celebration.

Let's Make It

Measurement: Hand-sized ● **Time:** ½ hour

MATERIALS

- Cardstock
- Old magazines and catalogs
- Foam paintbrushes
- Mod Podge
- Colored pencils, crayons, or markers
- Scissors
- Glue
- Single-hole punch
- New pencils or pens (you will need one per person)

TRACE AND COLLAGE THE TURKEYS

1 Have your kids place an open hand on cardstock and trace around the shape of their hand (fingers and all) with a pencil. Make one per person.

2 Look through old magazines and catalogs to tear out bits of seasonal colors. Encourage your kids to look beyond the objects to see the colors represented in the images.

③ Use a foam paintbrush to apply a thin coat of Mod Podge to each hand.

④ Collage the torn pieces of seasonal color on each hand however you like and apply another coat of Mod Podge. Allow to dry completely.

PERSONALIZE THE PLACE CARDS

⑤ Have your kids write each person's name on small torn paper pieces in contrasting colors. Apply each name directly onto a hand in the same manner you collaged it.

⑥ Carefully cut out each hand from the collage.

⑦ Use the hole punch to make a hole in the thumb and pinky.

⑧ Insert a new pencil through the holes coming from behind so the place card rests on the pencil.

⑨ As people find their seats at dinner, have your kids invite everyone to write down something they are thankful for on the back of their place cards, and then go around the table to share them with one another.

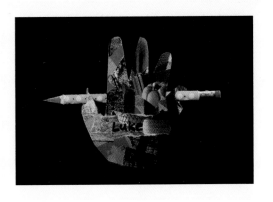

Felted Wool Marbles

Felting wool balls is a simple process and lots of fun. When you combine different colors of wool, you can create one-of-a-kind woolen marbles. Learn how to make them and then use your handmade marbles to create unique napkin rings that can easily be transformed into a cheerful garland or whimsical jewelry. My kids love making these and constantly come up with new ways to play with them. Roll up your sleeves and get ready for a new favorite family pastime.

Let's Make It

Time: ½–1 hour

MATERIALS

- Towels
- Mild soap or baby shampoo
- Wool roving in a variety of colors
- Blunt-tipped embroidery needle
- Embroidery floss or fishing wire

MAKE THE FELTED WOOL MARBLES

1. Set out plenty of towels on your work area.

2. Add a spoonful of soap to a large bowl and fill it halfway with very warm water.

3. Take the wool roving (a) and gently tear 3"–4" lengths of the fiber (b).

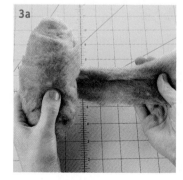
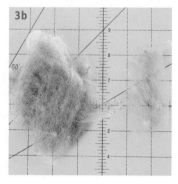

4. Place a few lengths of roving crossways on top of one another in your hand.

5. Roll the roving into a tight ball. Dip it into the soapy water to wet the fibers.

6. Remove the ball from the water and begin gently rolling it in your hands. It will feel a bit loosey-goosey at first, but soon the fibers will mesh together naturally, and you will feel the wool ball getting smaller and tighter as you roll.

7. Add more lengths of fiber and dip the ball back into the soapy water as you continue the process of gently felting the wool ball, layering different colors if you like. (It is best to use very warm soapy water, so change out the water as needed.)

8. When you are happy with the size and density of the ball, rinse it in cool water and then apply light pressure while rolling to coax out excess water.

9. Allow your wool marbles to dry on a towel.

USE YOUR MARBLES

10. String a blunt-tipped embroidery needle with a 12" length of embroidery floss or fishing wire. Tie a knot about 2" from the end.

11. String your wool marbles onto the floss, piercing through the center of each with the needle. (You could make a knot in between each one so that if the string breaks, they do not all topple onto the floor.)

12. When you have about 7" worth of the felted wool marbles all strung up, tie off the ends to form a tight circle.

13. Make a bunch to create a set of one-of-a-kind napkin rings. Kids will enjoy slipping their napkin rings onto their wrists as cheerful bracelets.

14. Use your leftover napkin rings to create a festive ringed garland for your home by simply joining them with embroidery floss.

Advent Tree as Big as Me

Go big with your advent calendar this year by turning a simple tomato cage on its head to create a tree as big as your kiddo. Stitch together 24 simple leaf pouches to add color, texture, and dimension to the tree. And when the little ones aren't looking, slip small gifts or secret messages into each of the leaves as a token to celebrate each day of advent.

Let's Make It

Measurement: Approximately 3' tall ● **Time:** 1 hour

MATERIALS

- 33" tomato cage (with three legs and three rings)
- Duct tape
- Extra-loft batting (craft size 36" x 45")
- 1 yard of dark green felt (72" selvedge)
- Chalk
- Scissors
- Low-temp hot glue gun
- 1 yard each of three shades of green felt (36" selvedge)
- Green embroidery floss
- Blunt-tipped embroidery needle
- Sticky-backed hook and loop dots

MAKE THE TREE

1 Turn the tomato cage upside down and hold the three legs together to create a tree shape. Duct-tape the tops of the legs together so no sharp points remain.

2 Unroll the batting into one big sheet and drape it over the top point of the tomato cage so that it extends a few inches past the bottom ring.

3 Wrap the batting around the cage to create a tree form. Smooth the surface as you go.

4 Once the entire tree form has been wrapped, tuck the batting under the bottom ring and secure it in place with hot glue or duct tape.

5 Lay out the 72" wide yard of dark green felt on your work surface. Place the tree form onto the felt, lining up the tree top with the corner and the longer edge.

6 Roll the tree in the felt and use the chalk to mark where the bottom of the tree form grazes the felt. The line will arc as you roll, creating a pattern piece similar to a slice of pie.

7 Remove the tree form and cut the pattern piece 2" outside the chalk line.

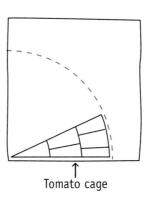

Tomato cage

8. Run hot glue along the bottom edge of the pattern piece and attach it to the tree form.

9. Stand up the tree form and wrap the felt around it to meet where you just glued. Cut it to overlap by 1" at the seam.

10. Hot-glue the pattern piece at the seam, working from the top of the tree downward.

11. Turn the tree upside down and wrap the excess felt under the bottom ring of the form, securing it in place with duct tape, hot glue, or by hand-sewing.

9

MAKE THE LEAF POUCHES

12. Have your kids place a hand onto a piece of scrap paper. Trace a leaf shape 1"–2" larger than the hand. This outline will be used as the pattern for your leaf pouches.

13. Fold each the three 1-yard pieces of green felt in half, creating a double layer of fabric.

14. Trace eight of the leaf patterns onto each double-layered fabric. You will end up with 48 pieces—16 in three different shades of green.

14

15. Use green embroidery floss and a blunt-tipped needle to hand-stitch two matching felt leaves together around the edges, leaving the top of each leaf unstitched to create a pouch.

16. Repeat to create 24 total leaf pouches.

15

ADORN THE TREE

⑰ Place a sticky-backed hook and loop dot on the back of each leaf pouch. You could also hand-sew a few stitches through each dot to attach them to the felt more securely.

⑱ With the tree standing upright, pin each of the leaf pouches around the tree in a manner that is pleasing to you. This step will help you determine placement of the leaves before you attach them.

20

⑲ Once you have decided where you want the leaves placed, apply the corresponding hook and loop dots to the tree form accordingly. (Again, you may wish to hand-sew a few stitches through each dot to secure them to the tree form more permanently.)

⑳ Stick each of the leaves onto the tree with the hook and loop dots.

㉑ For advent, fill each of the leaves with a special treat, secret message, coupon for something fun, or other surprise.

Kids will enjoy the tree as a fun decoration in their room the rest of the year.

Woven Felted Wool Valentines

Peg looms are great for making potholders and rugs with loops of fabric—but they can be used for so much more. In this project, you and your children will weave on a peg loom using a single length of yarn. Then you will felt it in the washing machine, creating a soft and thick blank canvas to use as one-of-a-kind valentines. Kids will enjoy each step of this process, especially punching messages and designs in place with the needle felting tool.

By the way, these also make great coasters.

Let's Make It

Time: 1 hour

MATERIALS

- Peg loom (we used a 9-peg loom)
- Yarn (heavy worsted or bulky-weight 100% wool works best, but you can also use a blend of wool/mohair, or wool/alpaca)
- 1 index card
- Single-hole punch
- Crochet hook (we used size G-6)

- Zippered lingerie bag
- Mild detergent
- Needle felting tool
- Needle felting mat
- Wool roving or wool felt

PREPARE YOUR MATERIALS FOR WEAVING

1. Every loom is different, so you need to measure the yarn for your project. The simplest way is to wrap the yarn around the loom twice the number of pegs on one side. (For example, we did 18 wraps around this 9-peg loom.)

2 Make a bobbin for your yarn by folding an index card in half. Punch a hole in the folded card, slip the end of the yarn through the hole and tie it off in a knot, then wrap the yarn around the bobbin.

WRAP THE YARN ONTO THE PEG LOOM

3 Look at the top row of pegs of your loom. Leave the tail of your yarn outside the loom between the first and second pegs from the right. Bring the yarn down from the top and in between the corresponding two pegs on the bottom row. Wind it counterclockwise around the first pegs on the bottom and top.

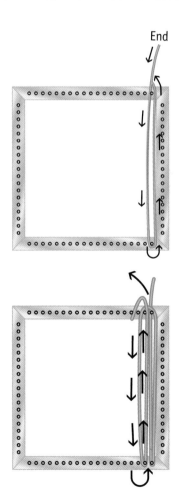

4 With the yarn back at the top, bring it over the second peg at the top, then down again. This time, around the second peg on the bottom, winding the yarn counterclockwise around the second peg.

5 The yarn is back at the bottom between the first and second pegs. Bring it back up, crossing to the third peg on the top. This time, wind the yarn counterclockwise around the third pegs on the top and bottom.

6. Repeat this sequence until you have wrapped all pegs top to bottom: Wrap counterclockwise, then cross to the next peg, wrap counterclockwise, then cross to the next peg, and so on.

7. End with the yarn at the top between the first and second pegs from the left.

WEAVE THE YARN THROUGH THE PEG LOOM

8. Pull the yarn around the corner to the side so that it is now between the first and second pegs on the side.

9. Weave your crochet hook, going under and over the "loops" of yarn. Hook a bit of the yarn while leaving the bobbin of yarn to the side. Pull the yarn with the crochet hook through, and loop it around the first peg.

10. Repeat this process using the crochet hook to pull "loops" of yarn and hook them over a peg. Each time you weave, go over where you previously went under, and under where you went over.

11. End with the yarn at a corner peg and tie a knot.

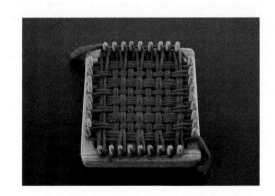

12. Don't worry if your finished pieces have some twisted loops, or if you haven't been precise about going over and under the exact same yarns every time. The fibers will tighten up considerably when you felt the pieces after they are off the loom.

13. Take your weaving off the loom. Use the crochet hook to remove the yarn loops one at a time. Pull the loop from one peg through the loop of the next one as you continue to remove them from the loom. (Most looms come with thorough instructions on how to do this step.)

⑭ Make a bunch of these woven squares before moving onto the felting stage.

FELT YOUR WEAVING

⑮ Place like-colored finished woven pieces in a lingerie bag and zip it closed.

⑯ Toss the lingerie bag into the washing machine with an old pair of jeans. Set the water level to low, the heat to hot, and the cycle speed to fast. Pour in a small amount of mild detergent to help with agitation.

Before   After

⑰ When both the wash and rinse cycles are complete, remove the felted wool pieces from the bag and flatten them to air-dry.

⑱ Trim off any excess threads or fuzz from the felted wool squares.

PERSONALIZE YOUR VALENTINES

⑲ Appliqué special messages to each of the valentines using a special needle felting tool and a needle felting mat.

⑳ You can form small bits of wool roving into hearts or various other shapes.

㉑ You can also cut out letters and shapes from 100% wool felt and appliqué those using the same process.

Use colored felt and heart-shaped pompoms to create this special heart-shaped wreath to adorn your front door this Valentine's Day. This project is sure to bring a smile to the faces of everyone who comes to visit.

Let's Make It

Measurement: Approximately 1'–2' in diameter ● **Time:** 1–2 hours

MATERIALS

- Heart-shaped wreath form
- Scissors
- Felt and yarn in valentine colors
- Low-temp hot glue gun
- Heart-shaped pompom maker

MAKE YOUR OWN WREATH FORM

Don't worry if you cannot find a heart-shaped wreath form such as the one suggested for this project. You can easily make one using simple materials from around the house:

- One wire hanger (made of a flimsy wire that you can easily bend by hand)
- Wire cutters
- Duct tape
- Bubble wrap or quilt batting

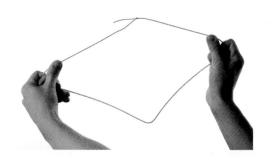

1. Cut off the hook part of the wire hanger, then smooth out all the bends in the wire.

2. Form the wire into a heart shape and twist the ends together. Apply some duct tape over the ends to cover any sharp points.

③ Wrap 3" wide strips of bubble wrap or quilt batting around the wreath form until you have created a thick and sturdy heart. Tuck in or tape the ends of the wrapping.

DECORATE THE WREATH

④ Cut 3" wide strips of colored felt that are long enough to wrap around and overlap a bit on the back of the wreath form.

⑤ Wrap a strip of felt around the wreath. Use the glue gun to secure it in place on the back of the wreath.

⑥ Continue to apply felt strips to the wreath, overlapping them a bit as you go, until the entire wreath is covered in a pattern that is pleasing to you.

⑦ Cut heart shapes out of colored felt.

⑧ Follow the manufacturer's instructions on the heart-shaped pompom maker to create a variety of colored pompom hearts.

⑨ Use the glue gun to attach a few of the heart-shaped pompoms to the wreath.

⑩ Glue different-colored felt hearts to the wreath in small groupings.

⑪ Loop some yarn around the heart and hang it on the front door of your home—your kids will know that home is where the heart is.

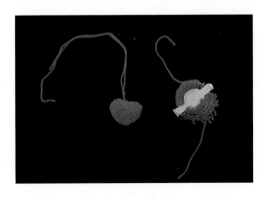

When your kids make their valentines this year, consider making something that friends and family can actually play with and keep. Kids will enjoy personalizing these puzzles with hidden messages and will get a kick out of their presentation. This project is a fun alternative to traditional valentines; however, you can easily reinterpret these puzzles for any occasion, making them as simple or challenging as you like.

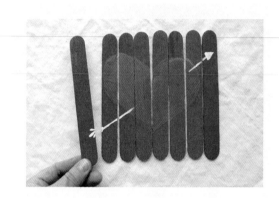

Let's Make It

Measurement: 6" x 6" ● **Time:** ½–1 hour

MATERIALS

- ¾" x 6" wood craft sticks (similar to tongue depressors)
- Painter's tape (masking tape is fine, too)
- Newspaper
- Acrylic paints
- Paintbrushes
- Ribbon, string, or twine

PREPARE YOUR WORK SURFACE

1. Set eight craft sticks side-by-side. Apply painter's tape across the top, middle, and bottom of the sticks to create a flat surface.

2. Place these sticks taped-side down on some newspaper (in case of spills).

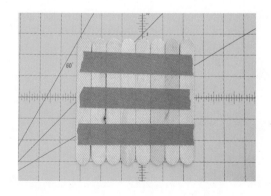

PAINT YOUR VALENTINES

3 Paint the entire surface of the sticks with a design that you like. Make sure that whatever image you paint extends across all of the sticks. The way the image is painted will provide clues for the recipient to assemble the puzzle.

4 Allow the painted surface to dry.

5 When the paint has dried completely, apply painter's tape directly to the painted surface across the top, middle, and bottom just as you did on the other side.

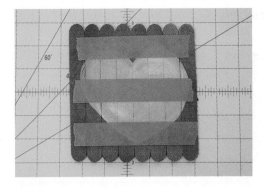

6 Flip the puzzle over and remove the tape from the unpainted side.

7 Paint a different design on this side of the puzzle. Use a different color palette on each side so that the recipient can use the colors as clues when assembling the puzzle.

8 Allow the painted surface to dry.

9 When both sides of the puzzle have been painted and are completely dry, remove the tape. Some sticks may be stuck together—simply snap the sticks apart.

10 Mix up the sticks in a random order, form a bundle, wind with some ribbon or twine, and present to the lucky recipient.

Egg Carton Ducklings and Bunnies

We all know that kids have the best imaginations. So let's encourage them to think outside the box—or outside the egg carton in this case. In this project, you will reuse an egg carton to create whimsical little pals. But please don't feel limited to ducklings and bunnies—you can easily adapt this project to create robots, aliens, or an entire zoo full of little animals.

Let's Make It

Measurement: Approximately 2" each ● **Time:** 1 hour

MATERIALS

- Empty cardboard egg carton
- Scissors
- Low-temp hot glue gun
- Colored tissue paper
- Mod Podge
- Small foam paintbrush
- Felt scraps
- Googly eyes (optional, but fun!)

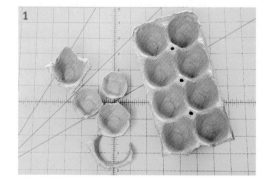

PREPARE THE FIGURES

1. Cut out all of the rounded cup-like sections from the bottom of your egg carton.

2. Cup two of them together and use the hot glue gun to attach them to one another.

3. Repeat this with all the egg carton cups—a one-dozen carton will yield six finished figures.

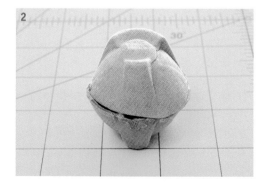

DRESS THE DUCKLINGS AND BUNNIES

④ Tear the tissue paper into 1"–2" pieces.

⑤ Use the foam brush to apply a thin coat of Mod Podge to a figure.

⑥ Place a piece of the tissue paper on the figure and then apply another thin coat of the Mod Podge. Don't worry, it will dry clear.

⑦ Continue layering pieces of the colored tissue paper until the entire figure has been covered and you no longer recognize it as part of an egg carton.

⑧ Cut out beaks, webbed feet, and bunny ears from the felt scraps—see page 236 in the Appendix for patterns or create your own.

⑨ Set your figures down to determine at which angle they will sit best. (We set the bunnies on the flat bottoms and set the ducklings on one of the side angles.)

⑩ Use a small amount of hot glue to stick googly eyes to the sides of duckling heads and the front of bunny faces. (Instead of googly eyes, you can make really cute eyes by cutting small circles from felt.)

6

7

⑪ Attach feet to the bottom and ears to the top of the bunny using a small amount of hot glue. (You can use craft glue instead, but we prefer to use hot glue because it dries very quickly.)

⑫ Use a few drops of hot glue to attach the beak to each duckling's face and the webbed feet to its sides.

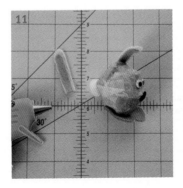

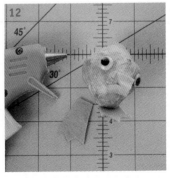

Color-Washed Newspaper Bouquets

You don't have to run to the store or even to the garden to put together a fresh-looking bouquet for someone you love. Just head to the recycling bin and grab some newspaper. Add a bit of paint, floral wire, and a few buttons to create a very special floral arrangement that will surely please the recipient—and it will never droop.

Let's Make It

Measurement: Approximately 5" in diameter ● **Time:** 1–2 hours

MATERIALS

- Dropcloth (optional, but helps with cleanup)
- Newspaper
- Acrylic paints
- Empty jars and cups (for paint)
- Foam paintbrushes
- Scissors
- Pre-wrapped (cloth stem) floral wire
- Buttons in a variety of sizes and colors

PAINT THE FLOWERS

1. Spread out single sheets of newspaper on your work surface. (You may wish to lay down a dropcloth underneath to simplify your cleanup.)

2. Mix a variety of color washes by diluting a teaspoon of acrylic paint with 1 ounce of warm water in empty jars. Stir to mix.

3. Apply the color wash onto the newspaper, covering each sheet almost to the edge. Be careful not to saturate the paper, because newspaper tears easily if it gets too wet.

4 Allow the painted pages to dry completely. If it is a nice day, leave them to dry in the sun to speed up the drying process.

5 When completely dry, paint the opposite side of sheet with a different color wash.

6 Allow the pages to dry completely.

FINISH THE FLOWERS

7 Cut 4"–5" circles out of the color-washed papers. These flowers look best if you cut imperfect circles of slightly different shapes and sizes.

8 Take one circle into your hand and gently squeeze and wrinkle it into a flower shape. Repeat this process with all the circles.

9 Stack three of these flower shapes one inside the other, varying the colors that appear on the outside and inside of each bloom.

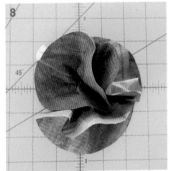

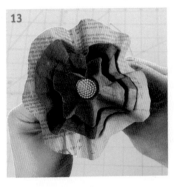

10 Take a 20" length of the cloth stem wire and thread both ends through a button.

11 Pierce the inside center of all three layers of the bloom with the ends of the wire and pull the wire all the way until the button is nestled in place at the center of the flower.

12 Thread another button onto the wire and pull it up to the bottom of the bloom to keep the wire from shifting and prevent tearing. Fit the flower snugly between the buttons.

13 Start under the flower right at the button and twist the two wires tightly until the entire stem of the flower is twisted together.

14 Once you have made a bunch of flowers, group 3–5 of them together. Wrap the stems together with ribbon or floral tape, if you like, and present the bouquet to someone special.

CHAPTER 7

Thanks Bunches

A great way to show family, friends, and all of your special people how much they mean to you is with a handmade gift. Whether it is small and simple, or incredibly detailed, knowing that it was made by your children will certainly be the very best gift of all.

Mind Your Beeswax Candles

Homemade rolled candles are a fun and easy project to do together. Learn a simple technique and add a dash of imagination to create magical one-of-a-kind candles, which make wonderful gifts and can also become a lovely tradition for family celebrations.

Let's Make It

Time: 10–15 minutes (or as long as you like)

MATERIALS

- Wicks
- Scissors
- Wax paper or a laminated place mat
- Beeswax sheets for rolling (8" x 8")
- Ruler
- Butter knife

MAKE ROLLED CANDLES

1. Cut a 2½" length of wick for a 2" candle.

2. Set a sheet of wax paper or a laminated place mat on your work surface to protect it.

3. Place a beeswax sheet onto your work surface. Use a butter knife and a ruler to cut a strip that measures 2" x 8".

④ Place the strip onto your work surface with the 2"
end closest to your body.

⑤ Set the wick onto the beeswax, about ¼" in from the
2" edge. The wick should be flush with one side and
extend ½" over the other side of the beeswax sheet.

⑥ Gently press the wick into the beeswax sheet. The
natural warmth of your hands will soften the wax
enough so the wick will stay put.

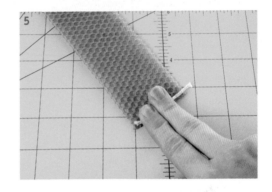

⑦ Use your fingers to work the ¼" edge of wax up over
the wick. You want it to be even and fit snugly
around the wick.

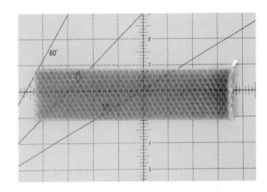

⑧ Slowly roll up the candle by rolling it away from
yourself. Pay attention as you go that the wax is
rolling straight.

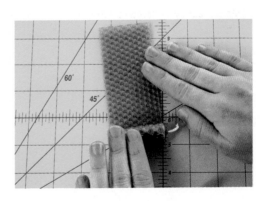

9. When you have rolled the entire 8" length around the wick and itself, you will have created a 2" taper candle.

10. Gently press the seam of the beeswax sheet into the candle with your fingers.

11. Once you are confident in this rolling technique, try making 8" taper candles using an entire beeswax sheet.

12. Make a whole bunch of colorful birthday candles using 2" squares of beeswax with 2½" wicks.

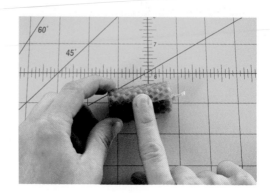

A set of hand-rolled beeswax tapers along with simple candlesticks make a lovely gift.

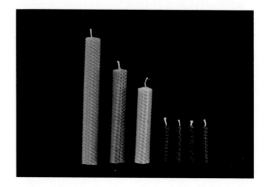

FAQ

Can we melt beeswax for dipped and poured candles?

Absolutely! You can use blocks of beeswax to create dipped birthday candles and even small poured candles. Try using household items as vessels, such as citrus fruit halves, nut shells, or empty glass candle jars.

There are a few safety precautions you need to take when melting wax. Have a fire extinguisher nearby and be familiar with how to use it. It is always best to be prepared—please discuss fire safety with your children in depth, and craft carefully. For detailed information about preparing wax and candle-making, visit your local library together to do some research before your next project.

Felted Wool Soaps

B undle some wonderful scented soap with colorful wool roving and take it for a little dip to create unique felted wool soap that is as lovely as it is useful. This project is fun and simple enough for even your youngest crafters.

Let's Make It

Time: 15 minutes

MATERIALS

- Towels
- Scented bar soap
- Butter knife
- Wool roving in a variety of colors
- Sheer stockings

MAKE THE FELTED SOAP

1. Set out plenty of towels on your work area.
2. Fill a bowl halfway with very warm water.
3. Cut a bar of soap in half using a butter knife.
4. Take a length of wool roving and gently wrap the fiber all the way around the bar of soap just like you would wrap a present.

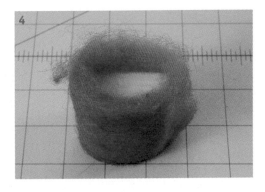

5 Take some more wool roving and wrap it around the bar of soap in the other direction, this time covering the ends that were not previously covered.

6 If small children are doing this project, place the roving-wrapped bar of soap into the leg of sheer stockings. Tie and cut off either end so that the soap is tightly wrapped in the stocking material. This step will help keep the roving from slipping around in little hands during the felting process.

7 Dip the roving-wrapped soap into the warm water to wet the fibers. Remove it and gently squeeze off the excess water.

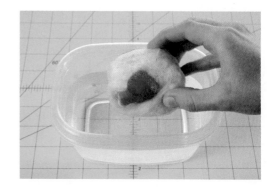

8 Gently begin to rub the entire bar of soap in your
   hands. It will feel like the roving is slipping a bit at
   first, but soon the fibers will mesh together naturally,
   and you will feel the wool getting tighter as you work.
   I can best compare this process to shaking dice in
   your hands.

9 The soap will begin to produce lather through the
   wool fibers, which will help the fibers to shrink and
   intertwine. If it gets too soapy, you can repeat Step
   7 to rinse it off a bit and continue felting again.

10 After a few minutes, you will feel that the roving has
   tightened around the soap and no longer slips. Rinse
   the soap with cool water and pat it with a clean
   towel to wick off any excess lather and water.

11 Allow the felted soap to dry on a towel.

12 Wrap a few soaps with a personalized note on handmade marbled paper (Chapter 3) for presentation.

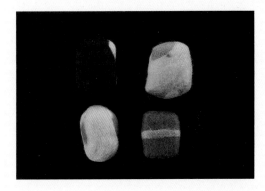

Peek-a-Boo Watercolor Cards

This beautiful one-of-a-kind stationery is made using everyday art supplies. Yours can be simple and understated or bold and bright by simply varying your color palette. Kids will enjoy seeing this project quickly come together and delight in presenting their creations to the special people in their lives.

Let's Make It

Measurement: 4¼" x 5½" • **Time:** ½ hour

MATERIALS

- Lightweight watercolor paper (9½" x 12½" or larger)
- Watercolor paints and paintbrushes
- A2 envelope (measures 4⅜" x 5¾")
- Scissors
- Pencil or pen
- Glue stick (or craft glue)
- A variety of paper craft punches, such as a single-hole punch and shape punches

MAKE A FEW WATERCOLORS

1. Paint a few pieces of watercolor paper in any manner you like. Whether you use a lot of color or keep it subtle, this project will work just fine.

2. Consider that each watercolor painting makes one card and envelope, so create enough paintings for as many cards as you plan to make.

3. Allow the paintings to dry completely.

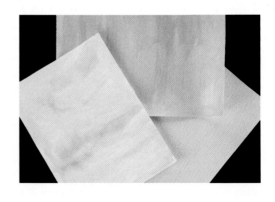

MAKE THE ENVELOPES

④ Carefully take apart the A2 envelope and unfold it completely. Use this envelope as your template.

⑤ Trace the envelope template on top of one of the watercolor paintings.

⑥ On that same watercolor painting, trace a rectangle measuring 4" x 5¼".

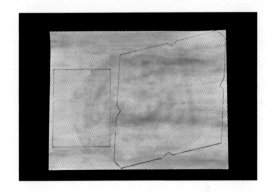

⑦ Cut out the envelope and rectangle shapes. Set the rectangle aside for use in the card.

⑧ Determine if you would like the painted side on the inside or outside of the envelope.

⑨ Fold both of the short sides of the envelope inward and crease firmly.

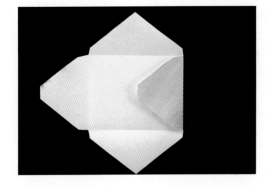

⑩ Fold the bottom upward and crease firmly.

⑪ Place a small amount of glue where the bottom of the envelope overlaps with the sides and glue in place. (You may wish to place a piece of wax paper inside the envelope just to be sure that no glue leaks inside the envelope and sticks it together.)

⑫ Allow the envelopes to dry completely.

CREATE THE CARDS

⑬ Cut some unpainted watercolor paper into pieces measuring 5½" x 8½". You will use one of these per card.

⑭ Fold each piece short end to short end and crease firmly along the fold.

⑮ Use different paper punches to create holes or other shapes on the front side of each card.

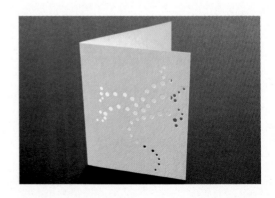

16 Place a thin layer of glue over the entire inside of the front of the card.

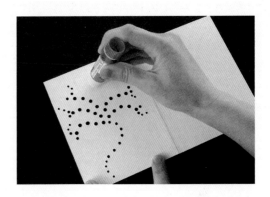

17 Take the 4" x 5¼" rectangle you cut out earlier and glue it face down inside the card. Center it so that the painted image peeks out of the holes. Smooth the paper with your hands to work out any air bubbles.

18 Allow the card to dry completely.

19 Package a few coordinating cards and envelopes together to give as a gift.

TIP

Repurpose Your Kids' Artwork

You can easily adapt this project to incorporate artwork already made by your kids. Cut out the cards and envelopes from plain watercolor paper or cardstock according to the previous instructions. When cutting out the rectangles of artwork to peek through the holes in the paper, simply choose from the wide array of artwork you have on hand by your kids. Even crayon scribbles and finger-painting by your youngest artists will translate into lovely stationery that will surely be treasured.

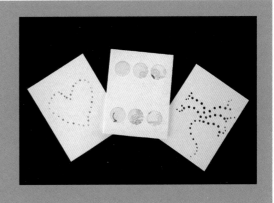

Name That Veggie Wrapping Paper

Look no further than your backyard garden or even the crisper drawer to create amazing printed wrapping paper. The process is fun for kids of all ages and produces unique results every time. Use your one-of-a-kind paper to wrap individual gifts—or better yet, bundle a few sheets to give as a thoughtful handmade present.

Let's Make It

Measurement: 30" x 30" ● **Time:** ½–1 hour

MATERIALS

- White or brown Kraft paper (30" wide roll)
- An assortment of vegetables such as celery, fennel, carrots, peppers, broccoli, artichokes, and cauliflower
- Cookie sheet
- Acrylic paints
- Empty small glass or plastic containers
- Foam brushes

SET UP YOUR WORK AREA

1. Cut a 30" piece of Kraft paper for each person and set it on the work area.
2. Select a few vegetables for printing.
3. Talk about the different ways the vegetables can be used to print on the paper (as brushes stamps, rollers, and so on).

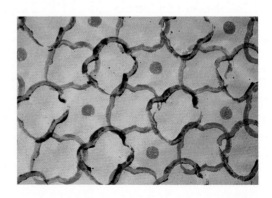

④ Make any cuts you would like in the vegetables and set all the individual pieces on the cookie sheet.

⑤ Determine your palette and squirt a few different colors of acrylic paints into individual small glass or plastic containers.

⑥ Place individual foam brushes beside each of the paint containers.

START PRINTING

⑦ With a small amount of paint on a foam brush, apply a thin, even layer to the surface of one of the vegetables.

⑧ Put down the brush and bring the vegetable over to your sheet of paper.

⑨ Press, brush, or roll the vegetable onto the paper and see what design you come up with. Experiment with color combinations and compositions as you go.

⑩ Continue printing on the paper until you are happy with the finished piece.

⑪ Set the paper aside to dry.

⑫ Try creating a paper printed entirely with one vegetable, but in different colors.

⑬ A fun idea would be to print with a variety of vegetables and write multiple-choice questions about the vegetable prints with a permanent marker.

Wildflower Gift Garden

A tiny garden of wildflowers can brighten any day. This project is as simple as planting a few seeds in a container, setting it in a sunny spot, and watching them grow. As the seedlings mature, transplant them into your outdoor garden or give them to someone special to brighten his or her day.

Let's Make It

Time: 15 minutes plus a few weeks growing time

MATERIALS
- Empty vessels for planting, such as milk or orange juice cartons, egg cartons, coffee cans, berry quarts, and yogurt containers
- Small pebbles (optional)
- Potting soil
- Wildflower seeds
- Spray bottle filled with water

PREPARE THE GARDEN FOR GROWING
1. Clean the vessel you will be using.
2. If using a large container with a solid bottom, place about an inch of small pebbles in the bottom for drainage.
3. Fill the vessel with potting soil, being careful not to press down the soil.

④ Sprinkle a thin, even layer of wild-flower seeds on top of the soil.

⑤ Gently press the seeds so that they are in contact with the soil, but not submerged.

⑥ Use a spray bottle to lightly moisten the seeds with water.

⑦ Set the container in a sunny spot and moisten the seeds as needed to germinate.

⑧ Continue to nurture the tiny garden until seedlings develop in a few weeks.

WRAP THE GARDEN FOR GIFTING

⑨ Wrap a piece of decorative paper around the vessel. Use some of your marbled paper (Chapter 3) or veggie wrapping paper (in this chapter).

⑩ Give the tiny wildflower garden to someone special to transplant in his or her own garden. Be sure to include care instructions, including what type of sun exposure the flowers require. And if you are feeling extra-crafty, include a personalized garden marker (Chapter 3).

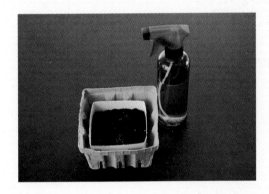

TIP

Mini-Gardens Make Great Gifts

Fill the cups of an empty egg carton with potting soil and plant a few different seeds in each cup.

Create a chart of which type of flower is in each of the cups and glue the chart on the inside of the carton lid—like a box of chocolates.

You can also create a mini herb garden by placing different herb seeds in each cup of the egg carton.

These make thoughtful gifts for Mother's Day or for your child's teachers at the end of the school year.

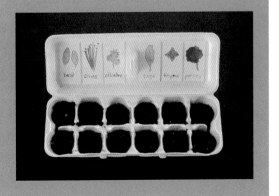

Woven Woolies

Weaving on a peg loom is a simple and fun process to teach your kids. In this project, you will do the little over-under dance with bulky wool and combine your finished squares to create a variety of cozy woolen pieces to share with others.

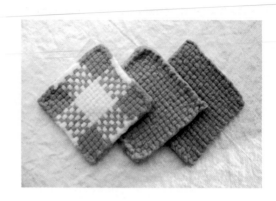

Let's Make It

Time: 15 minutes–½ hour per square

MATERIALS
- Peg loom (we used a 17-peg loom)
- Bulky-weight wool yarn (100% wool, or a blend of wool/mohair or wool/alpaca)
- Crochet hook
- Zippered lingerie bag
- Mild detergent

PREPARE YOUR MATERIALS
1. Make sure you have enough yarn for your project. We needed about 24 yards of bulky-weight yarn to complete one square using our particular loom.

WRAP THE YARN ONTO THE PEG LOOM
2. Tape a 3" tail of your yarn to the outside of the loom between the first and second pegs from the right on the top row.

3. Bring the yarn down in between the corresponding two pegs on the bottom row. Wind the yarn counterclockwise around the first peg on the bottom and then go back up.

End

④ With the yarn back at the top to the right of the first peg, bring it over the top of the first and second pegs, so that you can go down between the second and third pegs.

⑤ Bring the yarn down from the top again and in between the corresponding two pegs on the bottom row. Wind it counterclockwise around the second peg on the bottom and then back up to the top.

⑥ Continue winding the yarn onto the loom, working counterclockwise one peg at a time (as shown in the illustration). When you are at the end of the row of pegs, cut the yarn a few inches longer than needed and tape the yarn tail to the side of the loom.

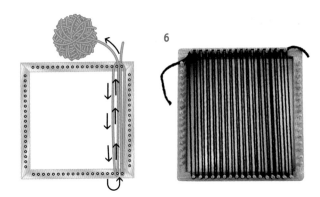

⑦ Look at the loom with those wraps of wool running vertically.

⑧ Double up the end of your yarn for a length of about 18". Starting on the left, pull the loop over 2 and under 2 across the entire loom until you are able to loop it over the top peg on the right side.

⑨ Knot the short-tail end of the yarn over the top peg on the left side.

⑩ Bring the yarn down over the second peg on the left and work a loop of the yarn under 2 and over 2 (the opposite of what you did on the previous pass) across the entire loom until you are able to loop it over the second peg on the right side.

⑪ Even out the yarn by giving it a tug from the left side and even out the line of weaving with your fingers.

⑫ Continue working in this manner. When the loom is fully woven, tie a knot in the yarn around the last peg.

13 Now it is time to take your weaving off the loom. Use the crochet hook to remove the yarn loops one at a time. Pull the loop from one peg through the loop of the next one as you continue to remove them from the loom. (Most looms come with thorough instructions on how to do this.)

FELT THE SQUARES

14 Before you go any further, please note that many things can affect the felting outcome. The type of yarn you use and tightness of your stitches have a lot to do with it, as does the temperature of the water and level of agitation. Do a test run with one of your squares first to see how much it will shrink during the felting process. Write down the measurements so you can calculate future projects.

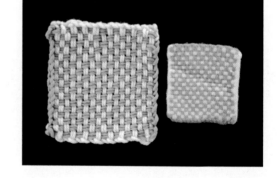

15 Place a finished woven piece in the lingerie bag and zip it closed.

16 Toss the lingerie bag into the washing machine with an old pair of jeans. Set the water level to low, the heat to hot, and the cycle speed to fast. Pour in a small amount of mild detergent to help with agitation.

17 When the wash and rinse cycles are complete, remove the felted wool piece from the bag and flatten it to air-dry.

18 Trim off any excess threads or fuzz from the finished piece.

19 Compare measurements of the finished piece with those of the pre-felted piece and do your calculations.

MAKE COOL STUFF WITH ALL THOSE SQUARES

One felted square makes a lovely trivet.

We stitched together six squares using the same yarn and then felted them to create color-blocked place mats.

You can join 9–12 squares to make a super-soft and especially cozy floor mat. (Set down a nonslip rug liner underneath to prevent falls.)

TIP

If you are up for a long-term project, make several dozen squares and put them together to create a one-of-a-kind woven wool patchwork blanket.

CHAPTER 8

Let's Party!

Half the fun of a party is in the preparation, and kids love to help. Work together on these projects to assemble a variety of fantastic party favors ahead of time—or better yet, select one special project to organize as a fun party activity. All your kids' friends can get involved in making their own favors to bring home and enjoy.

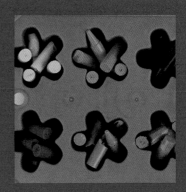

Itty-Bitty Book-in-a-Box

Combine your kids' love for all things miniature with their fondness for drawing by creating these itty-bitty matchbox sketchbooks. They are perfect for doodles and store away for safe-keeping in their own boxes.

Let's Make It

Measurement: 2⅛" x 1⅜" x ½" ● **Time:** 15 minutes

MATERIALS

- Matchboxes
- Newspaper
- Acrylic paint and paintbrushes
- Decorative papers
- Craft knife and self-healing mat, or scissors
- Ruler
- Glue or glue stick
- White drawing paper
- 2 small binder clips
- Stapler

DECORATE THE MATCHBOX

1. Remove the interior drawer from each matchbox and safely dispose of the matches. Protect your work surface by laying down a piece of newspaper.

2. Paint all sides of the interior drawer from each matchbox and set it aside it to dry.

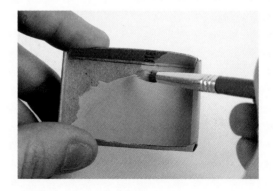

③ Cut a 4½" x 2⅛" piece of decorative paper.

④ Spread a small amount of glue all over the back of the piece of decorative paper.

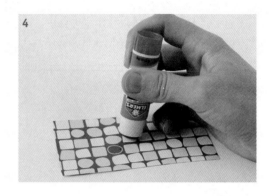

⑤ Apply the decorative paper to the outside of the matchbox, smoothing out any air bubbles with your fingers as you go.

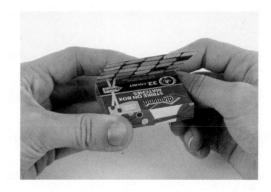

MAKE THE BOOK

⑥ Cut a 4" x 1¼" piece of decorative paper.

⑦ Cut 6–8 pieces of white drawing paper also measuring 4" x 1¼".

⑧ Fold the decorative paper in half short end to short end and crease along the fold.

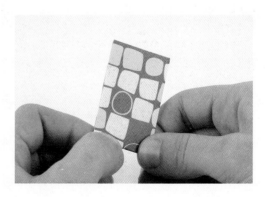

⑨ Unfold the decorative paper.

⑩ Stack the papers with the decorative paper as the cover facing out on one end of the stack. Line up the pages as straight as possible and secure both sides with small binder clips.

⑪ With the outside of the stack facing out, secure one staple through the center crease. This step creates a pamphlet binding on the book.

⑫ Fold all the papers of the book in half short end to short end and crease along the fold.

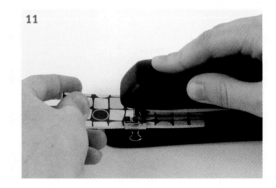

PUT IT ALL TOGETHER

⑬ Place the book in the drawer. (If necessary, trim the pages of the book to fit the drawer.)

⑭ Slide the drawer into the matchbox.

Dress up boring old pencils with decorative papers, glue, craft materials, and a few snips of your scissors. Work together with your kids to create a bunch of these pencils to share with friends and teachers at school.

Let's Make It

Time: 15 minutes+

MATERIALS

- Ruler
- Wooden pencils
- Decorative papers
- Scissors
- Glue or glue stick

- Single-hole punch
- A variety of fun craft materials such as pompoms, googly eyes, craft foam sheets and cutouts, felt, pipe cleaners, embroidery floss, and beads
- Tape

MAKE PAPERED PENCILS

1. Measure the pencil from the eraser hardware to the end. Cut a 1½" wide strip of decorative paper to that length.
2. Apply glue to the back of the paper strip.

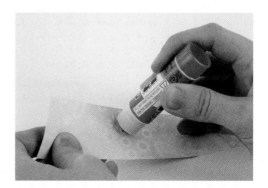

3 Apply the strip of paper to the length of the pencil starting at the eraser hardware.

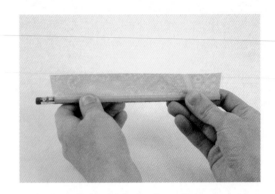

4 Carefully roll the pencil in the paper, smoothing it to the surface of the pencil and pressing out any air bubbles as you go.

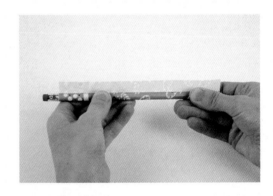

5 Apply a little bit more glue to the edge before you finish wrapping the paper onto the pencil, if needed.

6 Press along the edge of the paper down the length of the pencil to secure it in place.

7 Allow it to dry before sharpening for use.

CREATE MONOGRAMMED PENCILS

We used craft foam for these personalized pencil toppers, but they would also be great made with felt.

8 Punch two holes in a craft foam circle just inside the edge on opposing sides.

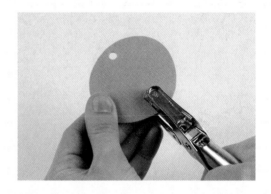

9 Cut out your first initial in a corresponding color of craft foam, or use a self-adhesive craft foam letter.

10 Apply the foam letter to the foam circle.

11 Slip the pencil through the two holes on the circle so that the letter is facing outward.

MAKE FRINGED PENCIL TOPPERS

12 Cut a 2" square of double-sided decorative paper.

13 Use scissors to cut slits in the paper, leaving ¾" uncut at the bottom edge.

14 Wrap the paper around the eraser hardware at the end of the pencil.

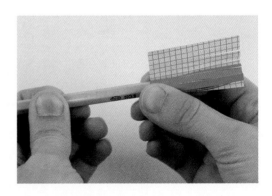

⑮ Tape the fringed pencil topper to itself, but not directly to the pencil. This way it can be easily slipped off when your kids need to use the pencil eraser.

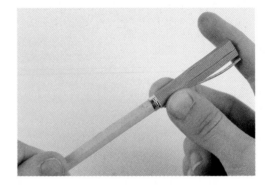

TIP

Create Your Own Pencil Pals

Set out a variety of materials and allow the kids to use their imagination to create their own pencil pals. Look in books and magazines for inspiration.

There really is no wrong way to do this project—have fun and encourage your kids to bring their designs to life.

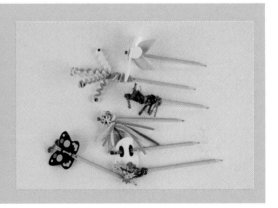

Driveway Doodlers

Drawing all over the driveway is great fun for kids of all ages. The next time your supply of chalk is running low, try making your own instead of purchasing yet another bin of the mass-produced stuff. In just a few minutes, you and your kids can mix up a batch in fun shapes and all your favorite colors.

Let's Make It

Time: 15 minutes plus drying time

MATERIALS
- Cookie cutters
- Duct tape
- Rubber gloves
- Empty bucket
- Plaster of Paris
- Long spoon or painter's stir stick
- Tempera paint powder
- Ice cube trays

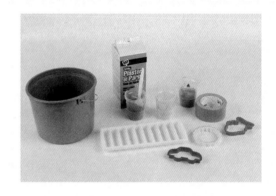

PREPARE YOUR WORK SPACE AND MATERIALS
1. Work in a well-ventilated area to protect everyone from plaster and paint dust.
2. The mixture will harden very quickly, so it is best to have all of your materials ready before you begin.
3. Cover one side of each cookie cutter with duct tape. Be sure it is well sealed.

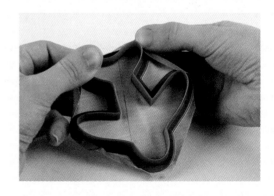

CREATE YOUR OWN CHALK

④ Wear rubber gloves when you work.

⑤ Combine two parts plaster of Paris and one part water in a bucket. Try 1 cup of plaster to ½ cup water the first time so you can familiarize yourself with the process.

⑥ Stir well to mix.

⑦ Add tempera paint powder to the mixture 1 table-spoon at a time and stir well to combine. Add more paint if needed to achieve your desired color.

⑧ Pour or spoon the plaster mixture into your cookie cutter molds or ice cube tray.

⑨ Allow to harden and dry completely. It can take anywhere from ½ hour to overnight, depending on the size of the chalks you create. The larger the pieces, the longer they will take to harden.

⑩ Unmold the chalk and enjoy!

Silhouette Charms

This fun twist on a classic silhouette portrait is a great way to chronicle the ones you love. These sweet little charms can be made into jewelry or sized to create memorable holiday ornaments.

Let's Make It

Measurement: About the size of a quarter ● **Time:** ½ hour

MATERIALS

- Profile photos of your kids (wallet-sized)
- 8" x 10½" sheets of artist's grade shrink plastic (such as PolyShrink)
- Sandpaper (fine grit)
- Scissors
- Single-hole punch
- Colored pencils
- Cookie sheet
- Baking parchment paper
- Clear sealer

PREPARE YOUR MATERIALS

You may wish to make a photocopy of each child's profile photograph so the original is not marked.

1 Follow the manufacturer's instructions to sand one side of a shrink plastic sheet. (If your shrink plastic is pre-sanded, you can skip this step.)

2 Choose one of the charm templates from pages 232–233 in the Appendix and trace it onto the shrink plastic with a pencil.

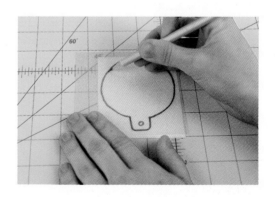

③ Use scissors to cut out each charm. You can also use decorative-edged craft scissors for a unique finished look.

④ Punch a hole in the top of each charm with a single-hole punch in the spot indicated on the template.

CREATE THE SILHOUETTE

⑤ Place the shrink plastic charm piece (sanded side up) on top of the portrait and trace with a black colored pencil. Set the portrait aside when done.

⑥ Use colored pencils to color in the entire silhouette shape. Traditional silhouettes are done in black, but feel free to use any color you like.

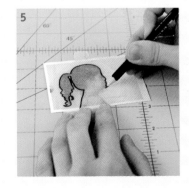

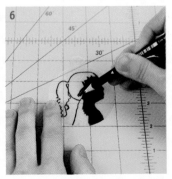

⑦ Write the date and the child's name or initials on the charm to make note of when this particular portrait was created.

SHRINK THE CHARMS

⑧ Space out the shrink plastic silhouettes on a cookie sheet lined with parchment paper.

⑨ Bake according to manufacturer's instructions to shrink the plastic charms. This is a quick process and really fun to watch through the oven door.

⑩ Allow the charms to cool completely.

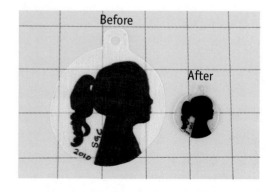

Before

After

FINISHING

⑪ Apply a coat of clear sealer to the charm to protect the silhouette from smudges.

⑫ String up your silhouette charm on a length of silk cord to wear as a necklace.

A simple charm bracelet filled with your family's silhouettes would be a fantastic gift for a mother or grandmother.

Another fun idea would be to create a much larger version of these silhouettes to make keepsake Christmas ornaments. Simply enlarge the charm templates as well as the photos you trace by 200%–300%.

Silhouette Charm Kits

Put together a kit of this project as party favors so your friends can make them at home after the party.

Follow steps 2–5 to prepare a few blank charms for each friend. Enclose a package of colored pencils and a small card with directions on creating the silhouette, as well as baking instructions.

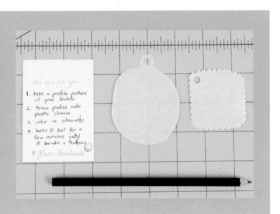

TIP

Easiest Play Dough Ever

Right in your very own cupboards are the ingredients for a terrific antidote to the "I'm bored" syndrome. Have the kids whip up a batch of this no-cook play dough and watch them become inspired to play and enjoy getting lost in their creations.

Let's Make It

Measurement: Approximately 1½ cups of dough ● **Time:** 15 minutes (plus hours of play time)

MATERIALS

- Mixing bowl
- Whisk
- Measuring cup
- Salt
- Vegetable oil
- Flour
- Food coloring

MAKE THE DOUGH

1. In a mixing bowl, whisk together ½ cup of salt, ½ cup of warm water, and ¼ cup of vegetable oil for about 5 minutes.

2. Add ½ cup flour to the mixture and continue to whisk until it forms a smooth paste. Continue to whisk for a minute to allow the salt to continue to dissolve and distribute.

3. Add another ½ cup of flour to the mixture and continue to whisk until it forms a smooth, sticky dough.

4. Sprinkle some flour onto your work surface and scoop the dough out of the bowl onto your work surface.

5. Knead the dough with your hands.

6. Add up to an additional ¼–½ cup flour as you knead until the dough is smooth and no longer sticky.

7. Divide the dough into a few smaller portions.

8. Flatten a small portion of dough and add a few drops of food coloring. (Fold over the dough so the food coloring does not drip all over your work surface.)

9. Knead the dough for a few minutes until it is your desired color.

10. Repeat steps 1–9 to create a colorful variety of dough balls, and enjoy!

177

Salvaged Scribblers

Almost everyone who has children has crayons in the house. And if you have crayons, you most likely also have a whole lot of broken crayon bits. Let's rescue those colorful pieces from certain fate in the garbage can by recycling them into colorful, whimsical crayons that the kids will love to use and share with friends.

Let's Make It

Time: ½ hour (plus cooling time)

MATERIALS

- Old crayons
- Vegetable spray
- A variety of whimsical molds such as silicone ice cube trays and mini-muffin tins
- Cookie sheet
- Toothpick or bamboo skewer (optional)

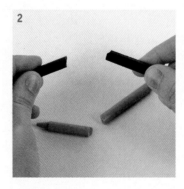

PREPARE YOUR MATERIALS

1. Peel any remaining paper wrappers off of your old crayons.
2. Break the crayon into small pieces.
3. Determine if you would like to make multicolored or single-colored scribblers and sort the crayons accordingly.

CREATE THE SCRIBBLERS

④ Preheat the oven to 200 degrees.

⑤ Lightly spritz your molds with vegetable spray.

⑥ Place the crayon bits into the molds.

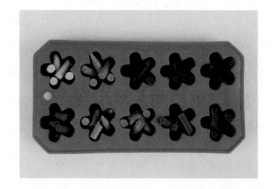

⑦ Put the molds on a cookie sheet and place the cookie sheet in the oven.

⑧ Melting the crayons is a relatively quick process, and the time is determined by the size of your molds. It might take anywhere from 5 minutes to 15 minutes. Watch through the oven door while the crayons melt.

⑨ Remove the cookie sheet and molds from the oven and allow them to cool completely before use.

⑩ If you are making multicolored scribblers, try swirling the melted wax with a toothpick or bamboo skewer to create marbled scribblers.

TIP

A few Salvaged Scribblers along with an Itty-Bitty Book-in-a-Box (instructions earlier in this chapter) would make a great party favor.

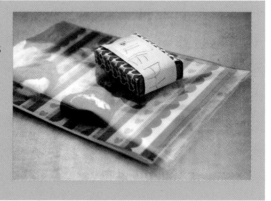

Add-a-Button Barrettes and More

Hair accessories featuring whimsical fabric buttons are a fun way for girls to express their personal style. In this project, you will learn the basic process and create a few special pieces that will allow your kids to switch the buttons as often as they wish.

Let's Make It

Time: 15 minutes (or as long as you like)

MATERIALS

- Needle nose pliers
- Cover button kit and cover button refill (available in the notions aisle of sewing and craft stores)
- Pen
- Small piece of clear hard plastic (a takeout salad container works great)
- Scissors
- Fabric scraps
- Self-adhesive hook and loop dots
- Barrettes
- ½" buttons with shaft
- Elastic ponytail holders and hair bands
- Embroidery floss or string

MAKE THE BUTTONS

1. Use needle nose pliers to remove the shaft from each of the button backs in the cover button kit.

2. Trace the button pattern from the cover button kit onto the piece of clear hard plastic to create a see-through template.

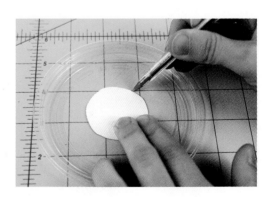

③ Cut out the template.

④ Use the template to trace the pattern onto fabric scraps, centering any desired images so that they appear centered on the buttons.

⑤ Cut out the fabric pieces.

⑥ Follow the manufacturer's instructions to secure fabric onto the buttons. Be sure to center any motif on the button prior to pressing it all together.

⑦ Apply a soft-sided self-adhesive hook and loop dot to the back of each fabric button.

MAKE ADD-A-BUTTON BARRETTES

8 Apply a scratchy-sided self-adhesive hook and loop dot to a barrette.

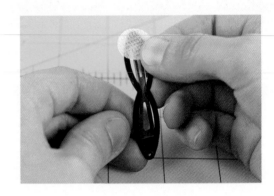

9 Apply a small scrap of fabric to the exposed adhesive on the reverse of the hook and loop dot (a) and trim it to size (b). Covering any exposed adhesive will help make sure it will not stick to the wearer's hair.

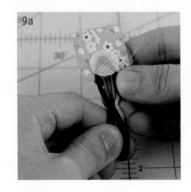

10 Secure any fabric button you like to the barrette by using the hook and loop dots.

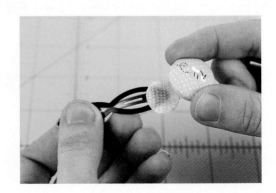

MAKE ADD-A-BUTTON PONYTAIL HOLDERS

⑪ Apply a scratchy-sided self-adhesive hook and loop dot to the face of a small button with a shaft.

⑫ Use a strand of string to pull an elastic ponytail holder through the shaft of the button.

⑬ Loop one end of the ponytail holder through the other to create a knot.

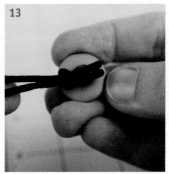

⑭ Secure a fabric button to the ponytail holder by matching the hook and loop dots.

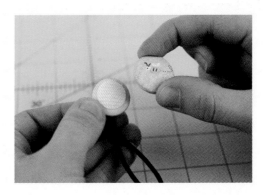

MAKE ADD-A-BUTTON HAIR BANDS

15 Apply a scratchy-sided self-adhesive hook and loop dot to the face of a small button with a shaft.

16 Use embroidery floss or string to tie the button to an elastic hair band.

17 Secure a fabric button of your choice to the hair band by matching up the hook and loop dots.

OTHER WAYS TO USE FABRIC BUTTONS

Glue small round magnets to the back of fabric buttons.
Once the glue is dry, you can use the buttons on your
fridge or magnetic memo board.

Fabric buttons make fun pushpins for your bulletin
board. Apply thumbtacks to the back of fabric buttons
with a small amount of glue and allow it to dry
before using.

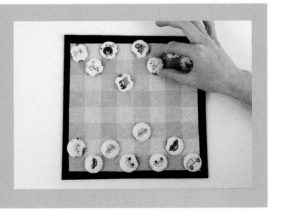

TIP

How About a Game of Checkers?

Glue felt to the back of fabric buttons and use
them as game pieces for checkers, backgam-
mon, and board games.

You can make this simple checkerboard by
applying a piece of large gingham to felt using
fusible web.

No-Trouble Bubbles and Wands

Everybody—young and old—loves bubbles. Let's whip up a batch of homemade bubbles and create your own personalized bubble wands.

Let's Make It

Time: 15 minutes

MATERIALS

- Wax paper
- Oven-bake polymer clay (we used Sculpey Soft)
- Alphabet rubber stamps with ¼" letters
- Baking parchment paper
- Cookie sheet
- Bucket

- Dishwashing liquid
- Serving spoon
- Measuring spoons
- Glycerin (found in the beauty aisle, or ask at the pharmacy counter at your local drugstore)

MAKE THE BUBBLE WANDS

1. Set out a piece of wax paper on each person's work surface.

2. Break a 2-ounce block of oven-bake clay into four equal-sized pieces.

3. Take a piece of clay and roll it into a log shape.

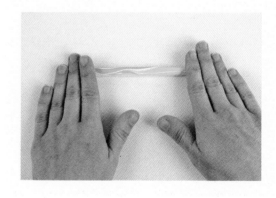

4 Create a loop in each end of the clay wand. Try a circle on one end and a different shape on the other—triangles, squares, and even elongated ovals will all work well for blowing perfectly round bubbles.

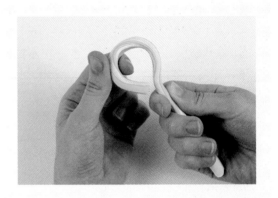

5 Use the alphabet rubber stamps to "write" your name on your wand.

6 Place the bubble wands on a parchment-lined cookie sheet and bake according to the manufacturer's instructions. They will shrink slightly and harden quite a bit.

7 Allow the bubble wands to cool completely before using them with your bubbles.

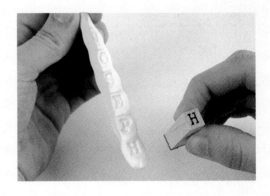

MIX THE BUBBLES

8 In a bucket, gently stir together 4 parts water to 1 part dishwashing liquid.

9 Add 1 tablespoon of glycerin for every 2½ cups of bubble mixture. Stir to combine.

10 The kids can use their new bubble wands with this mixture right out of the bucket.

11 You can also decant the bubble mixture into smaller containers (such as yogurt cups) for individual use.

8

9

12 This bubble mixture gets better over time, so make extra to fill a large bottle and allow it to "cure" for a few days.

CHAPTER 9

Game Time

Treat your family to some fun new boredom-busters. Nothing fancy is required, and you will spend little to no money. In this chapter, you will use what you have on hand and rethink materials from around the house. Enjoy the process of making these games together as you create a fully stocked game closet that is ready to provide entertainment all year round.

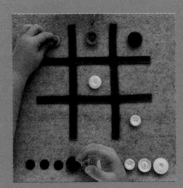

Upcycled Apartments

Even superheroes and the littlest of pets deserve a space of their own. Rather than purchase a premade house, let's transform items from the recycling bin to create a fun and fully furnished living space for your kids' favorite play figures. Everyone is sure to be entertained both during the design process and in the endless hours of imaginative play with the finished creations.

Let's Make It

Time: ½–1 hour

MATERIALS

- Empty tissue box
- Craft knife and self-healing mat, or scissors
- Acrylic paints and paintbrushes
- Balsa wood sheets or carpet samples
- Glue

- Decorative papers, maps, or magazines
- Cardboard (an old cereal box works great)
- Buttons
- A variety of craft materials such as yarn, felt, and fabric scraps

PREPARE THE APARTMENT SPACE

1 Cut the bottom off a tissue box.

2 Carefully remove any plastic in opening of the box. This opening will be the window.

3 Paint the interior of your apartment and allow it to dry completely.

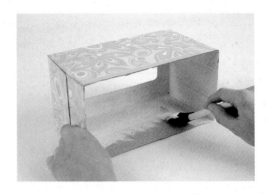

4 Measure the floor space and cut a piece of carpet or thin balsa wood to size.

5 Glue down your flooring.

6 Use your imagination and simple craft materials to decorate your space. Below are a few examples to get you started.

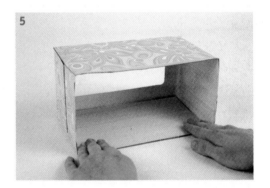

MAKE A COUCH

7 Cover a 3½" x 5" cardboard rectangle with fabric or decorative paper.

8 Look at the rectangle in the landscape position. Cut two 2" vertical slits in both sides of the rectangle that are placed ½" in and centered on either side.

9 Glue two buttons to the bottom of the couch.

10 Fold the rectangle long side to long side and crease on the fold.

11 Open the rectangle and pop the arms of the couch in the opposite direction.

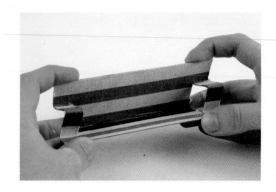

MAKE A COFFEE TABLE

12 Cover a 2" x 3½" piece of cardboard with fabric or decorative paper.

13 Fold both of the short ends about ¾" under at a right angle.

SPICE UP THE WALLS AND WINDOWS

14 Make frames around tiny pieces of art and maps to adorn the walls. Silhouette charms (Chapter 8) would look great on the walls, too.

15 Glue fabric curtains around the window.

16 Gather up a few play figures or make a few peg pals (see next project) to move into this great new space. Stack a few apartments to create your very own high-rise.

Peg Pals

This project is something the whole family can enjoy and it is sure to create lots of laughter. Craft your own wooden peg family or whip up an entire community—these figures are fun to make and provide countless hours of entertainment later on.

Let's Make It

Time: 1 hour

MATERIALS

- Wooden people pegs
- Painter's palette (or wax paper)
- Acrylic paints in an assortment of colors
- Old washcloth or paper towel
- Paintbrushes and cotton swabs
- Markers (fine-tip and wide-tip)
- Glue
- Scissors
- A variety of craft materials such as pipe cleaners, fabric or felt scraps, yarn, craft foam, stickers, and toothpicks

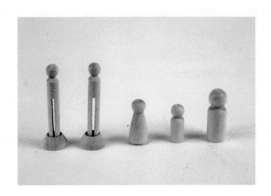

SET UP YOUR CRAFT AREA

1. Set out a few shapes and sizes of wooden people pegs to choose from while you work.

2. Use a painter's palette or some wax paper to mix your paints, adding a small amount of any given color at a time. You can blend right on the palette as you go.

3. Keep a cup of water and an old washcloth nearby for cleaning brushes as you work.

4. If you would like these to resemble specific people, gather a few photos for reference while you work.

PAINT YOUR PEG PALS

We like to keep our Peg Pals simple and add all sorts of accessories later, but you can get as detailed as you like.

5. Use a medium- or small-tipped paintbrush to paint "clothes" onto a peg person. You can make separates or one solid-colored article of clothing. Try adding stripes, polka dots, or different designs to each figure.

6. Allow the paint to dry before you handle the peg again.

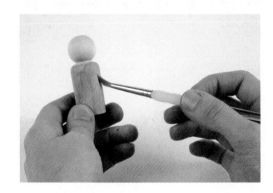

7. Now paint the hair. You can easily customize the hair color by mixing colors and using different-sized brushes. Try dabbing the paint on with cotton swabs to create curly hair.

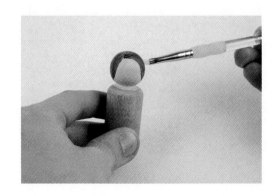

8. To add eyes, simply dab the end of the paintbrush without bristles into paint and dot eyes on the face area.

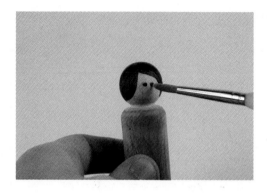

9. Use a fine-tipped marker or small-tipped paintbrush to draw a mouth.

10. Allow to dry.

TIP

Accessorize Your Peg Pals

Create a variety of accessories to personalize your figures. Attach them with glue when the paint is dry.

- Toothpicks are great for making drumsticks, batons, microphones, knitting needles, and so on. Use scissors to cut them to size. You may also wish to use a nail file to dull the sharp points.
- Cut small pieces of felt, craft foam, or stickers to indicate favorite sports and hobbies.
- Felt or fabric scraps make fun clothes, too.

Kaleidoscope

Watch as colors and shapes bounce around in this fun kaleidoscope. It is a great way for kids to discover how images and light can bend using a simple homemade prism.

Let's Make It

Measurement: Approximately 4½" tall ● **Time:** 1 hour

MATERIALS

- Cardboard toilet paper tubes
- Ruler
- Craft knife and self-healing mat, or scissors
- Granola bar wrapper with shiny silver liner
- Glue
- Clear plastic scraps (check your recycling bin for lids from yogurt cups, salad or takeout containers, etc.)
- Resealable plastic wrap
- Beads in a variety of shapes and colors
- Clear packing tape
- Black (or dark) paper
- Kids' original art (or decorative paper)

MAKE THE PRISM

1. Cut ½" off the length of a cardboard tube so it measures approximately 4" tall.
2. Cut the tube from end to end and flatten it to create a rectangle.
3. Fold the 4" edge of the cardboard over about 1¾" and crease on the fold.

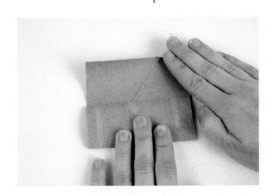

4. Fold the cardboard over 1¾" two more times, creasing on the fold each time. When you fold this piece together, it creates a triangular prism shape. (There will be a slight edge that overlaps the first side, which you will use later to glue it together.)

5. Open up the cardboard and glue the granola bar wrapper to it with the shiny silver side facing up. Smooth out any air bubbles with your hands.

6. Allow it to dry completely, then cut off any rough edges.

7. Fold up the cardboard with the shiny silver side on the inside of the prism.

8. Glue the prism together along the overlapping edge. Allow it to dry.

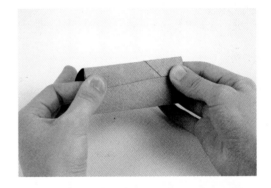

CUT THE PLASTIC

9. Stand up another cardboard tube.

10. Trace a circle onto clear plastic using the open end of the cardboard tube as a guide. You will need two of these circles.

11. Cut out the circles and set them aside.

ASSEMBLE THE KALEIDOSCOPE

⑫ Place the prism inside another tube that is taller than the prism, and push it all the way down to the bottom. There should be about a ½" gap above the prism at the top of the tube.

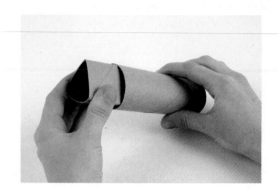

⑬ Place a piece of resealable plastic wrap sticky-side down on the top end of the tube.

⑭ Press down on the plastic wrap inside the tube with your fingers just to the depth of where the prism begins. (This step creates a "cup" inside where the beads will be placed.)

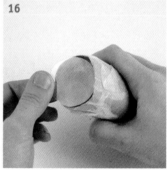

⑮ Smooth the plastic wrap up over the top outside edge of the cardboard tube and trim off any excess.

⑯ Take one of the clear plastic circles and place it inside the tube, creating a flat surface at the base of the plastic wrap "cup."

⑰ Place beads in different colors and shapes into the "cup" at the top of the tube. Do not pack the beads in too tightly, because they need to move around as you turn the kaleidoscope.

18. Place the second clear plastic circle on the top of the cardboard tube.

19. Secure it with a piece of clear packing tape, smoothing the edges down the sides.

20. Cut a circle out of black or dark paper. Use the opening at the prism end of the tube as a guide.

21. Secure the black circle onto the prism end of the tube with a piece of clear packing tape, smoothing the edges down the sides, just as you did with the top of the tube.

22. Use the point of a scissors to poke a tiny hole in the center of the black circle at the bottom of the kaleidoscope.

23. Press through that hole with a pencil and twist it around just a bit to create a small, round hole for viewing.

24. Measure the height and distance around your kaleidoscope.

25. Cut a piece of your kids' original art or decorative paper to size and glue it around the entire kaleidoscope.

26. Close or cover one eye as you look through the small hole in the end and turn the kaleidoscope to watch what happens as the beads move and are reflected in the prism.

Tic-Tac-Toe to Go

This classic pastime is simple enough for young kids to learn, and still fun for all ages. Rather than scribble on paper, create a special tic-tac-toe board to take along wherever you go. It is a wonderful diversion on car rides, in waiting rooms, or at restaurants, as well as a nice thing to bring along for play dates and visits to Grandma's house.

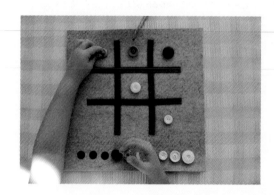

Let's Make It

Measurement: 12" x 12" ● **Time:** ½ hour

MATERIALS

- 1 piece of thick felt measuring 12" x 12"
- 4 strips of felt or ribbon measuring ½" x 8"
- Ruler
- Craft glue (such as Tacky Glue)
- 10 self-adhesive hook and loop dots
- 10 buttons (five each in two different colors)
- Screw punch or craft knife
- 1 piece of yarn measuring about 24"

MAKE THE GAME BOARD

1. Apply the four ½" x 8" strips to the thick felt with craft glue. The play area should be centered left to right, 1" down from the top and 3" up from the bottom.

2. Apply 10 scratchy-sided self-adhesive hook and loop dots to the game board at 1" intervals. Placement should be 1½" in from the sides and 1" up from the bottom edge.

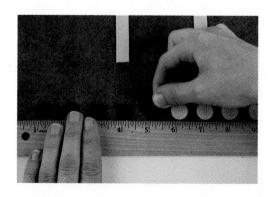

③ Stick the soft-sided self-adhesive hook and loop dots to your 10 buttons.

④ Secure the buttons to the game board using the hook and loop dots. This is where the game pieces are stored when not in use.

⑤ Use a screw punch or craft knife to make a small hole centered on the game board, positioned 1" down from the top.

⑥ Pull the piece of yarn through the hole. Tie a knot in both ends to prevent fraying.

Let's Play

- Place the board on a flat surface.

- Remove the colored buttons from the bottom of the game board for use when playing.

- When not in use, place the game pieces back onto the hook and loop dots across the bottom edge. Roll up the board from the bottom, wrap the yarn around, and tie it shut.

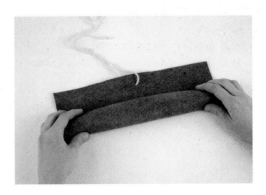

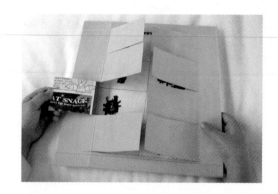

eing on the go with the kids in tow does not have to be stressful. Take a little time when you are not busy to work together and create a customized travel game to play in the car. Whether you are headed out of town on vacation or just up the street to visit friends, this game will make the ride something you will all look forward to.

Let's Make It

Measurement: About 9" x 12" ● **Time:** 1 hour

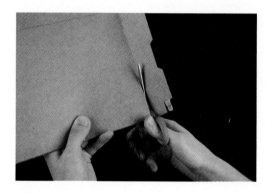

MATERIALS

- Empty cereal box (about 12" tall)
- Craft knife and self-healing mat, or scissors
- A variety of craft materials such as decorative papers, stickers, acrylic paints, and fabric
- Glue
- Ruler
- Pencil
- Plain paper measuring 8½" x 11"
- Colored pencils, crayons, or markers
- Ballpoint pen
- Clear packing tape

DECORATE THE GAME BOARD

1. Take apart the cereal box.

2. Trim off loose or rough edges to create a large flat cardboard rectangle.

3. Turn the cardboard over so you are looking at the plain "inside" of the box.

4. Decorate the cardboard in any way you like, such as painting, collage, or adding decorative papers or stickers.

5. Allow the game board to dry thoroughly.

PREPARE THE PLAY SHEETS

Do steps 6 and 7 in advance and then make a few photo-copies so that you have a supply of them ready for future use. That way you can speed through to the fun part.

6 Use a ruler and pencil to draw a 1" frame around the 8½" x 11" paper, measuring 1" in from all sides.

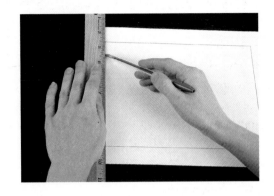

7 Divide the center space of the paper into eight equal-sized rectangles. (A simple way to do this step is to fold and crease the paper in half vertically and then again horizontally. This step creates four equal-sized spaces, which you can once again divide in half.)

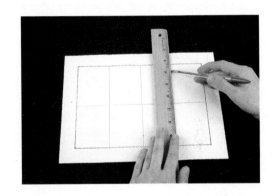

8 Brainstorm a list of things you might see while you are out and about in the car.

9 Draw images of these items in each of the spaces on your play sheet. Color them in and label them, if needed.

10 Once you have a few different play sheets, you may wish to make color copies of each so that the kids can play along together during a ride.

ASSEMBLE THE GAME BOARD

11. Place the cardboard piece with the decorated side facing up on your work surface.

12. Place a blank play sheet on top of one side of the cardboard.

13. Use a ballpoint pen to press around the lines and create an impression onto the cardboard.

14. Remove the paper and use those impressions as a guide to cut out eight flaps on one side of the cardboard.

15. Fold the cardboard in half with the decorated side facing out.

16. Use clear packing tape or colored duct tape to seal two of the three open sides of the game board.

Let's Play

- Insert one of the customized play sheets into the game board.

- Lift all the flaps on the game board so that you can see the items the kids are looking for while you play.

- As the kids spy things during the ride, they close the little flaps over those items.

- The first person to spy everything and close the corresponding flaps on the game board wins!

Floor Mat Hopscotch

Hopscotch is a terrific way to keep kids of all ages active, improve balance, and strengthen coordination. In this project, you will make a fun hopscotch mat that will be well-used for indoor play during the off-season.

Let's Make It

Measurement: 2' x 6' ● **Time:** 2 hours

MATERIALS

- Cotton duck canvas measuring 2' x 6'. (You can have yardage cut at the fabric store, or simply cut a piece to size from a cotton painter's dropcloth.)
- Tape measure
- Pencil
- Duct tape in a complimentary color
- Fabric paint
- Paintbrushes

MAKE THE HOPSCOTCH MAT

1. Use a tape measure and pencil in five horizontal lines at 1' intervals across the width of the canvas. See the illustration in the Appendix on page 234.

2. Measure and pencil in a 1' vertical line centered in the top section of the canvas.

3. Pencil in another 1' vertical line in the section that is third down from the top. See the illustration in the Appendix on page 235.

④ Cut or tear two 1' lengths of duct tape and apply them to the two vertical lines on the canvas.

⑤ Apply five 2' lengths of duct tape to the five horizontal lines on the canvas.

⑥ Use lengths of duct tape to bind the mat by wrapping it over all of the edges.

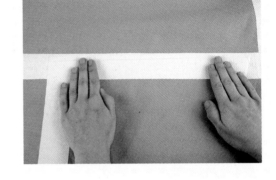

⑦ Lightly pencil in numbers 1–8 in the corresponding sections on your mat.

⑧ Paint in each of the numbers using fabric paint, following the manufacturer's instructions on how to set the paint.

⑨ Once the paint is dry and set, it's time to start playing!

A few crafts in this book would be great for tossing onto the hopscotch mat during play—try using fabric buttons (see page 180), beanbags (See page 75), or even a felted wool soap (See page 145).

TIP

Use a Nonslip Rug Pad on Hard Surfaces

Placing a nonslip rug pad underneath your hopscotch mat will prevent it from sliding around on hard surfaces, such as wood or tile floors.

Cut the nonslip rug liner to size and position it on the floor underneath the hopscotch mat, or permanently apply it to the hopscotch mat with spray adhesive.

Digital Scavenger Hunt

Combine modern technology with a traditional scavenger hunt in this fun activity. By using a digital camera, kids can gather items that might otherwise be impossible to access. This is a fun party activity, a clever game for long rides in the car, and a great way to collect memories during a family vacation or special occasion.

Let's Make It

MATERIALS

- 8 sheets of 8½" x 11" plain paper
- 1 piece of decorative paper or cardstock
- Single-hole punch
- Large tapestry needle (blunt-tip)
- Embroidery floss or yarn
- Pen or permanent marker
- Digital camera(s) (kid-friendly) or disposable camera
- Printer and photo paper (optional)
- Glue

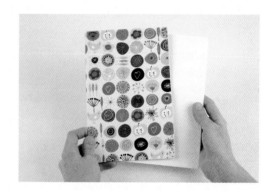

CREATE THE SCAVENGER BOOK LIST

1. Fold each piece of paper and the cardstock in half, short end to short end, creasing on the fold.

2. Slip the folded papers one inside the other to form a 16-page book and then slip the book inside the folded cardstock cover.

3. Make two holes along the spine of the book with a single-hole punch.

4. Use a tapestry needle to sew the book together through the spine with a few stitches of yarn or embroidery floss.

5. Brainstorm with your kids to create a list of items to find on the scavenger hunt.

6. Write one item at the top of each page.

START THE SCAVENGER HUNT

Kids can work in small groups or alone, depending on the number of kids and cameras you have. Just be sure the batteries for all of the cameras are charged and ready to go.

7. Review proper use of the digital cameras your kids are using.

8. Set parameters for the scavenger hunt as to how much time they have and any limits as to where they are to look.

9. Give each kid (or group) a scavenger list book and a camera, and send them on their way to "collect" each of the items.

SHARE YOUR FINDINGS

10. When the scavenger hunt is over, go through the photos on the camera and talk about what the kids found.

11. Print your kids' pictures either on your own printer or at a local drugstore.

12. Glue the photos in the book and encourage your kids to take even more photos to add to the book in the future.

TIP

Go on a Field Trip

Customize a scavenger list for your next visit to a museum or the zoo.

At the end of the day when you and your kids are back home, choose pictures to print and paste into their book as a special way to remember your adventure.

Nesting Family

Create a one-of-a-kind set of simple nesting dolls featuring your very own family. Use basic craft materials from around the house to personalize each character and bring your nesting dolls to life. Set them around the table as place cards at a family gathering or enjoy them as a fun element of imaginary play.

Let's Make It

Measurement: Up to 8½" tall ● **Time:** 1 hour

MATERIALS

- Portraits of family members (make photocopies to preserve the originals)
- Craft knife and self-healing mat, or scissors
- Cardstock (8½" x 11"—you will need one piece per family member)
- Ruler
- Fabric scraps, colored papers, or magazines
- Glue
- Markers, crayons, or colored pencils
- Duct tape
- Decorative tape or clear packing tape

CREATE YOUR NESTING FAMILY

1. Cut out everyone's head from the individual family member portrait copies.

2. Determine the order of how the dolls will nest together. You can arrange by age, height, or whatever order you wish.

③ One sheet of 8½" x 11" cardstock will be the first person.

④ Cut 1" off of both the length and width of the next sheet of cardstock for the second person. Cut 2" off of both the length and width of the next sheet of cardstock for the third person. Continue to decrease the size of the cardstock for each consecutive person. (If you have an exceptionally large family, trim the papers at ¾" intervals.)

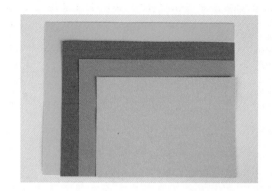

⑤ Glue each head centered along the top edge of its corresponding cardstock piece.

⑥ Cut out "clothes" and "accessories" from fabric, paper scraps, or magazines.

⑦ Glue the clothes and accessories onto each of the corresponding cards. Allow to dry.

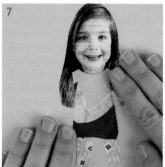

⑧ Use markers, crayons, or colored pencils to personalize each person as you wish. Include hobby items to further illustrate everyone's individuality.

9 Place the card face down and apply a length of duct tape along where the vertical seam will be when it is assembled.

10 Roll up the card with your person facing out. Overlap the edges by ¼" and secure along the seam using the duct tape that is now on the inside of the tube.

11 Apply a length of decorative tape or clear packing tape to the outside of the cylinder to secure that outside seam.

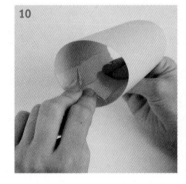

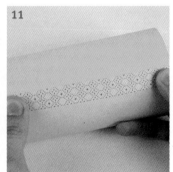

12 Repeat this process with each of your family members' dolls.

13 Nest one inside the other and have fun!

A fun way to bring your family's nesting dolls to life is by taping a wooden craft stick inside each character so they can be used as puppets. Try putting on a show using the tabletop puppet theater (see page 214).

Fridge Magnet Matchup

Transform the surface of your refrigerator into a game board with this simple and fun magnetic puzzle. Customize this game to feature your kids' photos, original art, or something as simple as pretty decorative paper.

Let's Make It

Measurement: 8" x 10" ● **Time:** 15 minutes

MATERIALS

- Photographs, artwork or decorative papers
- Inkjet magnet sheets (8½" x 11")
- Glue
- Ruler
- Pen
- Craft knife and self-healing mat, or scissors

CHOOSE YOUR IMAGE

1. If you are using a digital photograph, you can print an 8" x 10" image directly onto the white side of the inkjet magnet sheet using an inkjet printer. Allow the ink to dry completely.

2. If you are using original artwork or decorative papers, glue the paper image to the white side of the magnet sheet. Smooth out any air bubbles with your hands and allow it to dry completely.

CREATE THE PUZZLE

3. Use a ruler and pen to mark equal-sized puzzle pieces onto the magnet sheet. Consider the age of your kids when doing this—cut large pieces for little ones and smaller pieces for older kids.

4. Cut out the puzzle pieces and stick them onto your refrigerator in random order so the kids can get started solving their puzzles.

Tabletop Puppet Theater

Kids are so creative, and watching them put on a puppet show is one of the best forms of entertainment around. Encourage their imaginary play by creating this simple tabletop puppet theater using one of the greatest art materials around—a cardboard box. Make it your own and enjoy the show.

Let's Make It

Time: 1 hour

MATERIALS

- Empty cardboard box (we recycled a flat-rate priority mail box, but a cardboard box of any size will work just fine)
- A variety of craft materials such as decorative papers, stickers, acrylic paints, ribbon, and pompoms
- Glue
- Craft knife and self-healing mat, or scissors
- Felt or fabric (for the curtain)
- Ruler
- Stapler

CREATE THE PUPPET THEATER

1. Take apart the box.
2. Trim the box to create a flat cardboard rectangle. Cut off a long flap from one side and save it for use later.
3. Turn the cardboard over so you are looking at the plain "inside" of the box.

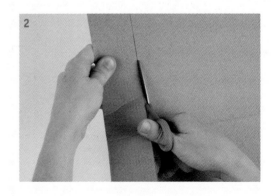

④ Decorate the cardboard any way you like, such as coloring or painting, collage, or adding decorative papers and stickers.

⑤ Allow any paint or glue on the cardboard to dry thoroughly.

⑥ Cut out a rectangle centered in the cardboard. This will be the stage area.

⑦ Cut a piece of fabric or felt for the curtain of your theater. It should measure slightly larger than the opening.

⑧ Place the fabric on the inside of the opening, then use a stapler to secure the curtain to the top edge.

⑨ Fold the box toward the back about 3" to either side of the opening. This step will allow it to stand up on its own.

10 If necessary, use the long piece of cardboard you cut off the box (in step 2) to create a brace that will help keep the theater in place. (Simply cut two corresponding slits in the bottom sides of the main "theater" and secure them over the long cardboard strip.)

11 Use ribbons, glitter, pompoms, and stickers to decorate the front of the theater in any way you like.

12 For performances, kids can tuck their hands under the curtain or simply drape the curtain over the top of the theater.

13 When not in use, remove the brace and fold the theater for easy storage.

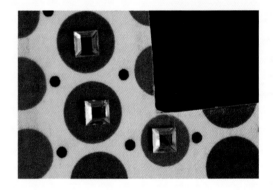

M usic is a universal language that can be appreciated by people young and old. Even the littlest kids respond to tones, pitch, and rhythm. Create a great starter set of band instruments by repurposing items from the recycling bin. They will get plenty of use and entertain the entire family.

Let's Make It

Time: ½–1 hour

MATERIALS

- Newspaper
- Fabric or felt scraps
- Rubber bands
- Cardboard tube from a paper towel roll
- Duct tape in a variety of colors

- Empty tissue box
- Toothpicks
- Small plastic comb
- Wax paper

MAKE A MICROPHONE

❶ Use your hands to tightly ball up 1–2 sheets of newspaper to the size of a baseball.

2. Wrap a piece of colorful fabric or felt around the newspaper ball. Gather the fabric tightly around the newspaper ball and secure it at the base with a rubber band.

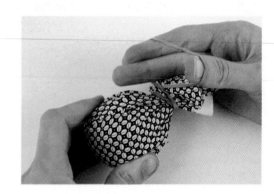

3. Place the secured end into the empty cardboard tube.

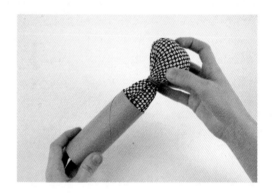

4. Wrap some colored duct tape around the end of the tube to secure the end of the microphone to the handle.

5. Roll up some newspaper and stuff it into the cardboard tube. This step will help to prevent it from being bent or crushed over time.

6 Continue to wrap colored duct tape down the length of the microphone in any pattern you like. Stop before you get to the bottom.

7 Place a small square of duct tape over the open end of the microphone and smooth the edges over the sides.

8 Continue wrapping the length of the microphone until it is done. Rock out!

TIP

Make Egg Shakers

Create fun percussion instruments by repurposing plastic Easter eggs. Fill plastic eggs halfway with rice, dried beans, or lentils. Close the eggs tightly and seal around the edges with tape. Different materials will result in different sounds—experiment and have fun.

MAKE A GUITAR-DRUM COMBO

9 Remove the plastic liner from around the opening of the tissue box.

10 Cover the box with colored duct tape in any pattern you wish.

11 Wrap 3–4 rubber bands around the box so they extend over the length of the opening. If you use rubber bands of varying widths, the resulting sounds will be different.

12 Place a toothpick or craft stick under the rubber bands close to the edge of the tissue box on either side. This will raise the "strings" ever so slightly and allow sound vibrations to resonate better.

NOTE: In the interest of safety, use string instead of rubber bands and omit the toothpicks if making this with very small children.

13 Pluck or pick the strings to play.

14 Flip the guitar over to use it as a drum!

MAKE A KAZOO

⑮ Cut a square of wax paper that measures the length of your plastic comb.

⑯ Fold the wax paper square in half and crease on the fold.

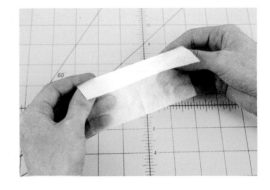

⑰ Slip the comb into the folded wax paper, positioning the teeth of the comb in the crease.

⑱ Use duct tape to seal only the top edge of the wax paper. The comb should be able to shift from side to side inside the wax paper, and it should not be tight.

⑲ To play, hold the kazoo by the duct-taped edge and place your fingertips on the ends of the comb. Try to avoid touching the wax paper if you can. Place your lips on the wax paper at the folded edge, take a deep breath and hum. Do not press your lips tightly on the comb; you are trying to create vibrations between the teeth of the comb and the wax paper. It may take a few tries and will be worth a belly laugh when you figure it out.

TP Tube 10-Pin

M ost kids jump at the chance to roll a ball and knock things down, so why not create your own bowling set using items from around the house? In very little time you can make a classic game that will entertain kids of all ages.

Let's Make It

Measurement: Pins measure about 4½" tall ● **Time:** 1–2 hours (including drying time)

MATERIALS

- 10 cardboard toilet paper tubes
- Duct tape (in any color you like)
- Sandwich wrap (such as plastic wrap, aluminum foil, or wax paper)
- Rice (dried beans or lentils also work well)
- Newspaper
- Clear packing tape
- Mod Podge
- Fabric or tissue paper in a variety of colors

MAKE THE PINS

1. Rip a piece of duct tape that is slightly larger than the end of a cardboard tube.

2. Place the tape over the end of the tube and smooth it onto the sides of the tube.

3. Bundle ½" cup of rice in a piece of sandwich wrap. Seal it so the rice does not leak out.

④ Place the bundle into the cardboard tube and push it down to
the end with the duct tape.
This step creates the weighted
base of the pin.

⑤ Fill the remaining space on top of
the rice bundle in the tube with
crumpled newspaper.

 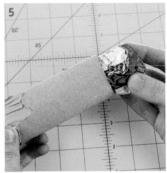

⑥ Place a piece of clear packing tape or colored duct
tape over the top of the tube and smooth the edges.

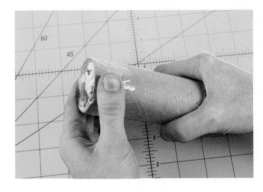

⑦ Apply a thin coat of Mod Podge to the cardboard
tubes.

⑧ Decorate the tubes in a variety of colors by layering
scraps of tissue paper. Create any design you like—
you can also cut pieces of fabric to size and glue
them around each of the tubes.

⑨ Apply a top coat of Mod Podge to the pins and allow
them to dry completely.

⑩ Set up the pins with the weighted sides down—we
used brightly colored duct tape to indicate the bottoms of the pins.

⑪ Find a soft ball in the toy bin and start playing!

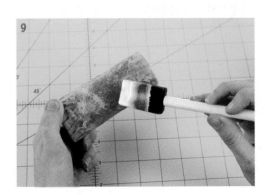

Story Puzzle Blocks

Kids of all ages enjoy playing with wooden blocks. And more than likely, you have some lying around the house. In this project, you'll update a few simple blocks by using them to create a special six-sided puzzle that will challenge everyone's thinking skills to put together colorful scenes from your kids' favorite stories.

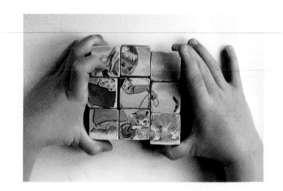

Let's Make It

Measurement: 3" x 3" x 1" ● **Time:** 1 hour (plus drying time)

MATERIALS

- Storybooks
- Clear quilter's ruler (optional)
- Craft knife and self-healing mat, or scissors
- 9 wooden blocks (measuring 1" each)
- Mod Podge
- Foam applicator
- Sandpaper (fine grit)

SELECT YOUR ARTWORK

1. Choose six images from favorite storybooks. It is helpful to use a quilter's ruler to visualize what will appear on the 3" surface of the puzzle. Consider color and composition when choosing your artwork.

2. You can select images from the same story, or select one each from several different stories. Scan and print (or make color copies) of the pages to be used on the puzzle.

CREATE THE PUZZLES

③ Cut a 3" square from one of the images.

④ Cut that 3" square into nine—1" squares.

⑤ Line up nine blocks to form a 3" square surface.

⑥ Use a foam applicator to apply a thin layer of Mod Podge to the top of each block.

⑦ Place each of the nine—1" square images on the top of a block.

⑧ Apply a top coat of Mod Podge directly on top of the pictures on each block, being sure to go over the edges of the images.

9. Repeat this process with each of the remaining five images, working one side at a time.

10. By the time you complete five surfaces on the blocks, the first side should be dry enough so that you can turn it onto that side to complete the sixth side of each block. If the surface is slightly tacky, you can place the blocks on a sheet of wax paper as you complete the final side.

11. Allow each block to dry completely.

FINISH THE BLOCKS

12. Use fine-grit sandpaper to sand and smooth the edges of each image on the blocks.

13. Apply a final top coat of Mod Podge to each of the blocks and allow to dry.

14. Place the blocks into a bowl for display when not in use.

TIP

Put on Your Thinking Cap

Encourage kids to use clues on each of the blocks to determine which sides should be facing in the same order.

Once you get the hang of these puzzle blocks, make more complex versions—use more blocks, incorporate text with the images, or try using photographs. A set of puzzle blocks made using photos of grandchildren would be a thoughtful gift for grandparents.

Reference Materials

I encourage you to support local businesses that specialize in art and craft supplies. In addition, the following resources offer materials referenced in projects throughout the book.

Clover Needlecraft, Inc.

13438 Alondra Blvd.
Cerritos, CA 90703
www.clover-usa.com
(needle felting tools and mats, pom-pom makers, rotary cutters, self-healing mats, craft notions)

craftsanity.etsy.com

Jennifer Ackerman-Haywood
(handmade wooden peg looms)

Dritz Brand—Prym Consumer USA Inc.

www.dritz.com
(button kits, cheesecloth, grommets, printable fabric, craft notions)

FilzFelt Inc.

300 A Street
Boston MA 02210
www.filzfelt.com
(100% wool felt)

Ornamentea
509 N. West St.
Raleigh, NC 27603
www.ornamentea.com
(wool roving, shrink plastic,
craft supplies)

Plaid Enterprises, Inc.
3225 Westech Dr.
Norcross, GA 30092
www.plaidonline.com
(Mod Podge, craft supplies)

A Child's Dream Come True
www.achildsdream.com
(wool felt, beeswax candle sheet,
wool roving)

Duck Brand Duct Tape
www.duckbrand.com

Jo-Ann Fabric and Craft Stores
www.joann.com

Michaels Stores, Inc.
www.michaels.com

Martha Stewart Crafts
www.marthastewart.com
(also available at Michaels Stores and Jo-Ann Fabric and Crafts Stores)

Etsy.com
(search for handmade craft supplies)

Templates

TRICK-OR-TREAT FORTUNE TELLER GAME TEMPLATES

Frankenstein

Jack O'Lantern

Ghost

Vampire

Spider

Wicked Witch

Bat

Black Cat

SILHOUETTE CHARMS TEMPLATES

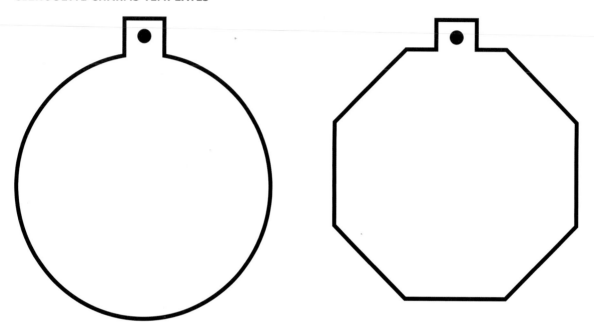

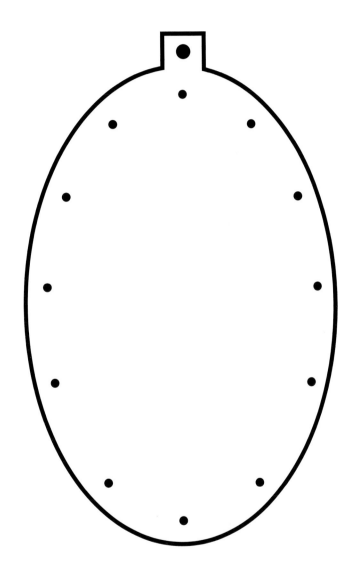

FLOOR MAT HOPSCOTCH ILLUSTRATIONS

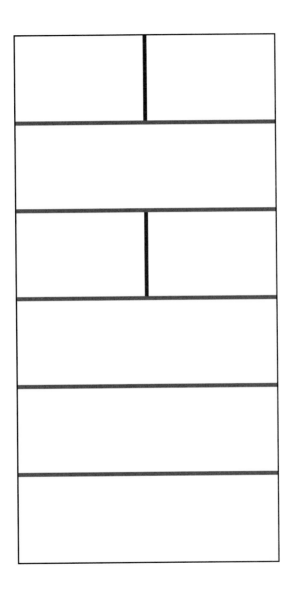

EGG CARTON DUCKLINGS AND BUNNIES TEMPLATES

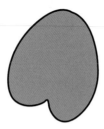

Bunny Feet

Bunny Ears
(Make 2 each)

Duckling Feet
(Make 2)

Duckling Beak
(Make 2)

Index

Yearning to do more with yarn?

Packed with photos, patterns, and step-by-step instructions,
you'll love knitting the visual way!

978-0-470-27896-3   978-0-470-07782-5   978-0-470-06817-5

Avai **31901050535378**